TOKYO FM Midtown Studio

六本木・東京ミッドタウンに来たら、
TOKYO FMのサテライトスタジオへGO！

イイ音は、イイ空間から生まれる。
イイ音は、イイ時間をつくる。そして、
イイ音は、イイオトナをつくる。
ココ六本木のオトナの空間からアナタの
ココロの真ん中へ。届けたい番組がある、
届けたい思いがあるTOKYO FMです。

六本木・東京ミッドタウン プラザ1F
○都営大江戸線「六本木駅」8番出口直結　○東京メトロ日比谷線「六本木駅」地下通路にて直結

TOKYO FM　Just Me, Just 80MHz

Mon-Thu
11:30〜13:45
(Fri 11:30〜12:55)
赤坂泰彦

A'll that RADIO

オトナの街から、
オトナの耳へ。

The sound of the word Africa makes people feel adventure. Most people feel that they would like to visit this mysterious and serene land once. The reason being, that the this magnificent nature born from the earth remains untouched. Everybody imagines a dream of exploring the jungle, as a child. The admiration for African savannas and jungles, does not change with adulthood. Many people perhaps resign themselves to visualizing the dream once in their life given the chance. However, if one tries to make the journey, it is not hard to step foot on the land of Africa. If one has a little courage and time to spare anyone can visit the African continent. This unimaginable encounter of this South African wild paradise is waiting for you, with the sea that has whales, penguins, and sea lions, and the land that has giraffes, elephants, and lions.
Now, with our hearts racing let's open the doors of the great nation of Africa that we have all dreamed of since we were children.

Dreamy voyage through South African design
夢の南アフリカ・デザインの旅

アフリカという言葉の響きは、人に夢とロマンを感じさせる。神秘的でおおらかなアフリカへ一度は訪れてみたいと感じている人は多い。
その理由は、地球の生まれたままの雄大な自然が残っているからであり、ジャングルを探検することは、子供の頃に誰もが想いをはせる夢であったからである。アフリカのジャングルやサバンナへの憧れは、大人になっても変わらない。ひょっとすると一生見続ける夢物語なのかもしれないとあきらめている人も多いだろう。
しかし、少し足を伸ばせば、アフリカの大地を踏みしめるのは難しいことではない。ほんの少しの勇気と時間の余裕を持てれば、誰もが訪れることができるアフリカ大陸。野生の楽園南アフリカでは、海では鯨、ペンギン、アシカ、陸ではライオン、象、キリンと想像以上の出会いが待っている。
さあ、胸を高鳴らせながら、子供の頃から夢見たアフリカの大地の扉を開けてみよう。

If you desire office in character with you,

あなたがあなたらしいオフィスを望むなら、

+PLUS
FURNITURE WORKSHOP

〒100-0014 東京都千代田区永田町2-13-5 赤坂エイトワンビル1F
TEL 03-5860-2350 / FAX 03-5860-2351
営業時間:平日 10:00～19:00 / 土曜 10:00～17:00
定休日:日曜、祝日、年末年始

http://www.shop-plusplus.jp/

+81 Voyage South Africa Issue

Contents

006-013	**World Travel Information**	
014-109	**South Africa**	
	016-028	Kuruger National Park
	029-047	Cape Town Landscape
	029-031	Table Mountain
	032-033	Cape Grace Hotel
	034-041	Cape Good Hope
	042-045	Cape Town Landscape
	046-047	Wine Land
	048-083	South Africa / Creator of Cape Town
	084-087	Johannesburg Landscape
	088-104	South Africa / Creator of Johannesburg
	105-109	Soweto
110-118	**Ecode**	
119-120	**Editor's Note & Credit**	

Voyage World Travel Information

BRAZIL

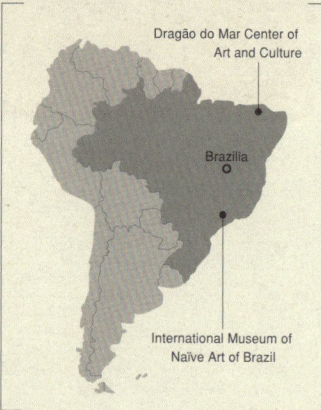

The Dragão do Mar Center of Art and Culture

複合文化センターDragão do Mar Center

The Dragão do Mar Center of Art and Culture is a multicultural arts and leisure complex located in Fortaleza, Ceara. Within this huge site, which spans 33,000 square meters, can be found a variety of facilities such as exhibition spaces, a playhouse, a cinema, and even a library. The highlight of the center however is the planetarium, which is supposedly the first in the world to allow visitors to experience observing the Milky Way through a German technique incorporating twenty multimedia projectors. There are also restaurants and bars, so one can easily enjoy an entire day here. The architecture is the work of Delberg Ponce de Leon and Fausto Nilo.

セアラ州フォルタレザにある、芸術と文化、レジャーの複合文化センターDragão do Mar Center of Art and Culture。33,000 m²という広大な敷地内には、展示会スペースや劇場、シネマ、図書館といった多様な施設が建設されている。また、世界一といわれるドイツの技術を用いたマルチ・メディア・プロジェクターを20機搭載し、本物の銀河を観測しているような映像を体感できるプラネタリウムは圧巻。もちろん、レストランやバーもあるため、1日中楽しむことができる。建築はDelberg Ponce de LeonとFausto Niloによるもの。

www.dragaodomar.org.br/index.php

Rio de Janeiro, I like you, I like your happy people

Artist Lia Mittarakis was born in Rio de Janeiro. Having lost her parents at the age of ten, she had her first encounter with oil painting while living in an orphanage. Her vivid paintings have been lauded by European critics as "painted poems". However, due to a retinal detachment she has lost the ability to see from her right eye, and her left eye can only see with 60 percent of its normal ability. Despite this, she continues to paint on due to her belief that "by painting the beauty of nature I can make the world remember that it is on the brink of a crisis". Her art can be found adorning the walls of the International Museum of Naïve Art of Brazil, which features works by artists from every province of Brazil as well as over 100 different nations dating back from the 15th century up to the present.

リオデジャネイロ生まれのアーティストLia Mittarakis。10歳で両親を亡くし、孤児院で生活していたとき油絵に出会う。彼女の鮮やかな作品は「描かれたポエム」とヨーロッパの評論家からも評されている。しかし、網膜剥離により右目の光を失い、左目も60%は見えなくなってしまうが、「自然の美しさを描くことにより、世界が危機にひんしていることを思い出させることができる」という信念のもと作品制作を行う。この作品は、ブラジルの各州で活躍する画家の作品から、近代から15世紀まで遡り100ヶ国以上から作品を集めたInternational Museum of Naïve Art of Brazilに飾られている。

www.museunaif.com.br

SWEDEN

text: Joachim Bergström from Embassy of Sweden

Head out! Take the train to a wonderful past
でかけよう！列車に乗ってすばらしい過去への旅へ

Picture by Joachim Bergström of Grön berså by Stig Lindberg

Picture by Joachim Bergström of Haparanda Stadshotell

Sweden – like much of the rest of the design world – is in a retrospective mood right now. Colors, shapes, and patterns from the 1950s and on resurface, and new designers draw inspiration from the past. Considering Japan's own 'Showa boom', and the love for the 'natsukashii', We are sure Japanese design lovers have much to do – and get – in Sweden. Of course you can find both newly-old series and vintage stuff in the big cities, but chances for real adventure increase if you board a train or rent a car, and head out into the countryside. Check guidebooks or local papers for 'Flea markets'! Usually held on the weekends, these popular places offer great design from past decades. How about some vintage Grön berså, or a 1974 chair by IKEA, or maybe some Orrefors classics? They might not come cheap – but things with a true soul never do.

デザインを誇る他の国々と同様、現在スウェーデンではレトロなムードが漂っている。1950年代に流行した色、形、パターンが再到来し、新人デザイナーたちは過去からインスピレーションを受け、新しいものを創作している。日本には独自の「昭和ブーム」があり、「懐かしさ」を愛する心を持っているので、日本のデザイン愛好家は、スウェーデンのデザインに共感し多くのものを得ることができるだろう。もちろん古いシリーズのリニューアル版や、ヴィンテージものは大都市で入手可能だが、列車に乗って、あるいはレンタカーを借りて田舎に行くと本当の冒険に出会う機会が増える。ガイドブックや地方紙などをチェックして「蚤の市」情報を調べてみよう。週末に開かれる人気の「蚤の市」では、過去の素晴らしいデザインを見つけることができる。Grön bersä（グレーンベショー）のヴィンテージもの、IKEA製1974式の椅子、あるいはオレフォッシュのクラシックはいかがだろう？値段は安くなくとも、本物の魂が込められたものばかりが揃う。

www.haparandastadshotell.se

While out in the country, I am sure you will need to take a rest. In smaller towns all over Sweden, classic 'Grand Hotels' are kept up and running – many as they always have been. Seemingly immune from change and the trend of the week, their lovely interiors are preserved, mirroring their status as centers of social life, royal visits, and business delegations over past decades. Check in, take a rest or head for a sauna before evening sets. Sit down over a quiet dinner: the white tablecloth is starched and pressed, the cutlery somewhat heavy, and the china strong but decorated. Pay attention to the sounds. The town's mayor might very well be sitting at the table next to you – or a minister from Stockholm visiting her constituency.

田舎へ足を延ばした時にも、休息は必要である。スウェーデンの小さな都市では、伝統的な「グランドホテル」が以前と同じように営業を続けている。現在のトレンドや変化に左右されることなく、独自の愛らしいインテリアを保っている。過去十年間に渡って王家やビジネス使節団が訪問していることからも、ずっと社会生活の中心にあることがわかる。チェックインして休息をとってもいいし、夕食の前にサウナに入ってもいい。糊のきいた白いテーブルクロス、重みのあるシルバー類、装飾が施されているしっかりとした陶器で、優雅な夕食を楽しめる。そして、周囲から聞こえてくる声にも耳を傾けてみよう。その町の市長、あるいはストックホルムに住んでいる大臣が選挙区を訪ねに来ていて、あなたの隣のテーブルに座っているかもしれない。

Picture by Kiyomitsu Maeda

As hard as I might try, after living in Japan for several years I could not describe Swedish food culture as close to wonderful. But lately, an interesting change has taken place, with fusion food surfacing on the plates: amazingly playful creations drawing inspiration both from an indigenous Swedish past and from abroad. But please promise not to leave Sweden without giving the classics a real chance. Head to Prinsen in central Stockholm! The friendly waiters will guide you through the menu – the traditional dishes have a depth and gracefulness you will not find anytime soon. Start out with Kalix löjrom; then go for the Biff Rydberg. Ask for the pepper grind – freshly ground pepper over egg yolk is your art project for the evening!

日本に数年間住んでいる僕にとって、スウェーデンの食文化を素晴らしいと表現するのは難しい。だが最近、スウェーデンの伝統と外国の食文化に影響を受けた、遊び心豊かなフュージョン料理が登場し変化が起きている。しかし、ストックホルムの中央にあるPrinsen（プリンセン）のようなクラシカルなレストランへ訪れることなくスウェーデンから離れないでほしい。店内ではフレンドリーなウェイターがメニューを説明してくれる。伝統的な料理は、他にはない深みと上品な味わいある。まずはKalix löjrom（カリックス・レイロム）、そしてBiff Rydberg（ビッフ・リードベリ）を食べてみよう。卵黄にかける挽きたての胡椒は今晩のあなたの芸術的な一品になるだろう。

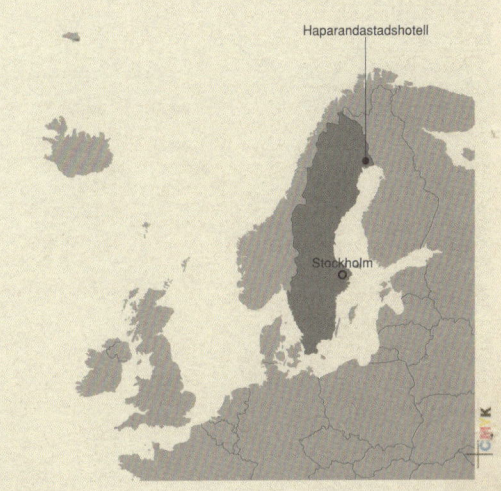

Haparandastadshotell

Stockholm

UNITED KINGDOM

ZAHA HADID @ Design Museum

Phaeno Science Center, Wolfsburg, Germany Zaha Hadid Architects 2005
Photographer: Werner Huthmacher

Vortexx Chandelier
by Zaha Hadid Architects for Sawaya & Moroni

DESIGN MUSEUM /
The Haymarket Hotel

The Turner Prize 2007

London

Photographer: Steve Double

The exhibition of Zaha Hadid, the architect from Baghdad, Iraq, held at the London Design Museum has been the subject of conversation for some time. Being one of the standard-bearers for deconstructivism in modern architecture, Zaha Hadid was named a CBE for her dynamic work throughout the world. She is an energetic architect and well known as the first woman to have won the Pritzker Prize in 2004. This exhibition covers a wide range of her works including rare drawings from her early years, her present and future works, models, paintings and interior designs. This is her first full scale solo exhibition in London and a golden opportunity for the audience to learn about her vision of the world.

ロンドンのDesign Museumで行われているイラク・バグダット出身の建築家、Zaha Hadidの展覧会が話題になっている。Zaha Hadidは、現代建築における脱構築主義の旗手の一人であり、世界を股にかけたダイナミックな活躍を評価され、大英帝国勲章（CBE）を受章。また2004年に女性として初めてプリツカー賞を受賞したことでも有名な気鋭の建築家だ。今回の展覧会では、初期の貴重なドローイングから、現在、そしてこれからの作品、模型、ペインティング、Hadidがデザインを手がけたインテリアの展示まで、多岐に渡る作品が盛り込まれている。イギリスでは初の大々的な個展となるため、彼女の世界観を知ることができる絶好のチャンス。

DESIGN MUSEUM
www.designmuseum.org
29th June 2007- 25th November 2007
2007年6月29日～11月25日

The Haymarket Hotel open
ロンドン発、最新デザイン・ホテル

The Haymarket Hotel opened in May this year as the hotel group's seventh property following the Soho Hotel, the much talked about design hotel in London. The Haymarket Hotel features distinctive interior design fusing contemporary and classic English style, and the luxury extends to the fifty rooms all individually designed and decorated. Superbly located right at the back of Trafalgar Square, it is worth noting that the hotel has a 18-m swimming pool with a lounge bar. The designer-made lightings illuminate the water surface creating an illusionary space.

ロンドンで話題となったデザイン・ホテル、Soho Hotelに引き続き、今年5月に同ホテルグループの7件目となるHaymarket Hotelがオープンした。コンテンポラリーなデザインと、英国のクラッシックなデザインを融合させた個性溢れる内装が特徴的で、全50室全てに違うデザインを施してあるという贅沢ぶり。特筆すべきは、トラファルガー・スクエアのすぐ裏という最高のロケーションにありながら18mのプールを所有していること。プールにはラウンジ・バーが併設されており、照明デザイナーが手がけたというライティングがプールの水面を照らし出し、幻想的な空間を演出している。

The Turner Prize 2007
ターナー賞 2007

©Damien Hirst
Mother and Child Divided 1993 Collection of Damien Hirst

©Gillian Wearing
Sixty Minute Silence 1996
Image courtesy Maureen Paley, London
colour video projection with sound 60 minutes

The Turner Prize is a contemporary art award that has been presented since it began in 1984. The Prize is usually held at Tate Britain but this year, the Turner Prize 2007 exhibition is being shown at Tate Liverpool. The four artists Zarina Bhimji, Nathan Coley, Mike Nelson and Mark Wallinger have been shortlisted and the winner will be announced at Tate Liverpool on 3rd December. A major retrospective presenting works by all the past winning artists, including Damien Hirst, Anish Kapoor and Gilbert & George, will be held at Tate Britain at the same time.

1984年以来、毎年イギリス国内の優れた現代美術作家に対して授与されるターナー賞。例年ロンドンのTate Britainで行われていたが、今年はTate Liverpoolで開催される。ノミネートされた最終候補者はZarina Bhimji、Nathan Coley、Mike Nelson、Mark Wallingerの4名で、受賞者の発表は12月3日に行われる。Tate LiverpoolとTate Britainで行われるターナー賞展では、過去の受賞者であるDamien Hirst、Anish Kapoor、Gilbert & Georgeなどの作品も展示される予定。

The Turner Prize 2007 exhibition
Tate Liverpool:
19th October 2007- 13th January 2008
Tate Britain:
2nd October 2007- 6th January 2008

回顧展
Tate Liverpool：2007年10月19日～2008年1月13日
Tate Britain：2007年10月2日～2008年1月6日

www.tate.org.uk/turnerprize

The Haymarket Hotel
Address: 1 Suffolk Place London SW1Y4BP
Telephone: + 44 (0)20 7470 4000
Price: Double room　£245～
www.haymarkethotel.com

SWITZERLAND

Plus Eighty One Voyage
World Travel Information

text: Switzerland Tourism www.myswiss.jp

A new spa with design by celebrated architect Mario Botta is born in Arosa's five-star Tschuggen Grand Hotel

アローザの5星ホテル「チューゲン・グランドホテル」に、有名建築家マリオ・ボッタのデザインによるスパが誕生

Boasting a history spanning over a century, the Tschuggen Grand Hotel is the premier five-star hotel nestled amidst the beautiful natural scenery of Arosa. December of 2006 saw the creation of the spa "Berg Oase", which was designed by Mario Botta, a renowned Swiss architect responsible for countless contemporary structures. The spa, whose name means "mountain oasis" in German, expresses a modern aesthetic in its use of glass. However, the shape of the building is like that of a tree's leaf for a design that blends smoothly into the surrounding forest. The spa is particularly uplifted by its illumination at night, which also enhances its illusion-like beauty. The newly expanded Tschuggen Grand Hotel has also just completed remodeling all of its 130 rooms, and has plans to be open during the 2008 summer season as well.

100年以上の歴史と伝統を誇る「チューゲン・グランド・ホテル（Tschuggen Grand Hotel）」は、美しい自然に抱かれたアローザの5星ホテルである。2006年12月には、スイス出身で数々のコンテンポラリー建築を手がける有名建築家、マリオ・ボッタがデザインしたスパ「ベルグオアーゼ（BERG OASE）」が誕生。ドイツ語で"山のオアシス"を意味する建物は、素材にガラスを用いモダンさを表現する一方、建物の形状は木の葉のようで、周辺の森に自然にとけ込むデザインとなっている。特に夜間はイルミネーションによって建物が浮かび上がり、その幻想的な美しさが強調される。今回、新たな発展をとげたチューゲン・グランド・ホテルは全130室の客室改装も終え、2008年からは夏期も営業予定。

www.tschuggen.ch

Bern's new destination, the Zentrum Paul Klee

ベルンの新名所「パウル・クレー・センター」

The Zentrum Paul Klee, which opened of June of 2005, is a large-scale art gallery housing nearly 40 percent (over 4,000 pieces) of the total works of Paul Klee, who lived half his life in Bern. Carrying on the will of Klee, who loved many aspects of culture from music to the arts, the Zentrum is more than just a mere gallery. In addition to a children's museum and music hall, it also contains a database library and restaurant, and serves as a multicultural center numerous workshops and events. Famed Italian architect Renzo Piano created the plan of the Zentrum. The bright design, which makes heavy use of glass and features a waved roof that resembles three mountains, stands out nicely within the spacious nature of its location, and the building is sure to be a spot of great interest for those with a passion for architecture.

2005年6月にオープンした「パウル・クレー・センター（Zentrum Paul Klee）」は、その半生をベルンで過ごしたパウル・クレー作品の約40％にあたる4000点以上を所有する大規模な美術館である。芸術、音楽など幅広い文化を愛したクレーの意思を継ぎ、単なる美術館ではなく、子供ミュージアムや音楽ホール、データベース・ライブラリー、レストランなどを併設し、複合文化センターとして多くのワークショップやイベントなどを開催している。センターの設計は、イタリア人有名建築家レンゾ・ピアノ。3つの山のような波形屋根とガラスを多く使って明るく仕上げたデザインは、周辺の広大な自然の中でひときわ目を引き、建築好きにも興味深いスポットだ。

www.zpk.org

Tschuggen Grand Hotel
Zurich
Zentrum Paul Klee

BLICKFANG TOKYO 2007

From Wednesday, October 31st to Sunday, November 4th, 2007, Japan's largest design event "Designer's Week" will be held in Meiji Jingu Gaien, Tokyo. In connection with this, a special tent will be set up at the interior products trade show "100% Design Tokyo" that will house "Blickfang", a design fair of European interiors, fashion, and jewelry. Blickfang will display an onslaught of items from nearly forty brands from mainly Switzerland, Germany, and Austria. Many of the designers themselves have also been brought to Japan, with their works available for purchase directly at the event. This year the sense of collaboration between the different countries has deepened, and the tourist bureaus for each of the nations will have booths on location. The Swiss National Tourist Office is also providing information about Swiss design.

2007年10月31日（水）〜11月4日（日）に東京の明治神宮外苑で開催される、日本最大のデザインイベント「デザイナーズ・ウィーク」。その一環で、インテリア・プロダクトを中心としたトレードショー「100%Design Tokyo」の会場内に特設テントを設け、ヨーロッパのインテリア、ファッション、ジュエリーのデザイン見本市「ブリックファング」が出展される。ブリックファングはスイス、ドイツ、オーストリアを中心とした躍進する約40ブランドの作品を展示、そのデザイナーも来日し、会場にて直接作品の販売も行われる。今年は各国とのコラボレーションを深め、会場内に各国観光局のブースを設置。スイス政府観光局もスイスデザインに関する情報を発信する。

100% Design Tokyo: www.100percentdesign.jp
Blickfang（ブリックファング）: www.blickfang.com

FINLAND

text: Shigeyoshi Noto from Finnish Tourist Board

Former prison is opened as new hotel in Helsinki
ヘルシンキに刑務所ホテル、Hotel Katajanokkaオープン

The capital of Finland, Helsinki has only a million population including surrounding areas, but several new hotels have been opened in last few each years. The most outstanding hotel opened this year so far is Hotel Katajanokka, which used to be prison. The location is quite convenient, close to Viking Line terminal, also only 10 minutes walk from market square. Of course it's surprising the prison was situated in heart of the city, but it's further unique to be renovated as hotel. This prison was seen in the movie, The Lights in the Dust directed by famous Finnish movie director, Aki Kaurismaki. Hotel Katajanokka is well renovated as modern hotel with full of light, but some memory is left on the wall with Graffiti. Also former prison residences returned as guests with special memory, which increased guardians just after opening. Hotel restaurant facing courtyard named Jailbird is one of the best recommendation, when it's sunny day. Why don't you stay as innocent prisoner.

フィンランドの首都ヘルシンキは、周辺部を含めても100万人あまりの人口ながら、ここ数年は年に数件のホテルがオープンするラッシュぶり。2007年前半の1番の目玉は「Hotel Katajanokka（ホテル・カタヤノッカ）」だろう。何せ場所は元刑務所。ロケーションはヴァイキング・ラインの発着港のすぐ近く、マーケット広場から徒歩10分という便利さ。こんな市の中心に刑務所があったこと自体驚きだが、それをホテルに改装するのもユニーク。この刑務所は、アキ・カウリスマキの敗者3部作の最終章「街の灯り」のシーンにも使われていた。現在は開放的で吹き抜けの明るい雰囲気だが、室内に受刑者の落書きが残っていたり、オープン直後には元受刑者が懐かしさのあまり泊まりに来るため、ガードマンの数を増やすなど話題になった。レストラン「Jeilbird（刑務所島）」では天気の良い夏には中庭席で、気持ちの良い白夜を楽しむことができる。あなたもこのホテルで受刑者気分を楽しんでみては？

Hotel Katajanokka information
Address: Linnankuja 5, Helsinki
Telephone: +358 9 686 450

The Kyoto tradition bridges Japanese culture and Finnish design
日本伝統文化が結ぶデザイン・コラボ始動

Oko (Incense) is Japanese traditional fragrance based on Buddhism, but it's used as tool for relaxation and healing nowadays. Lisn, one of the product line by Shoeido, which is incense shop based in Kyoto started the collaboration with Finnish designers followed by opening a shop in Helsinki July 2006. Finnish designers innovated new designs for incense holder and the designs are exhibited both in Finland and in Japan with the schedule as followed. Finnish design is often taken as one of the best combination with Japanese interior, let's see how it goes in incense.

お香といえば日本の伝統文化。近頃はリラックスやヒーリングのために利用する人も多いが、松栄堂（京都市中京区）が手がけるお香ブランドショップ「リスン」は、2006年7月のヘルシンキ進出に引き続き、若手フィニッシュ・デザイナーとのデザイン・コラボを開始した。日本・フィンランド両国でエキシビションを開催し、フィニッシュ・デザイン発のインセンスホルダー（お香立て）を展示する。予定は以下の通り。北欧デザインがどのようにお香をとらえるのかに期待が膨らむ。

Lisn to Finland exhibition information
Lisn Kyoto 25 Oct-14 Nov Cocon 1F, Shijyou-Karasuma, Shimogyou-ku, Kyoto
Axis Gallery 27 Oct-4 Nov Axis Bldg. 4F, 5-17-1 Roppongi, Minato-ku, Tokyo

リスン京都 10月25日（木）〜11月14日（水）　京都市下京区烏丸通四条下ルCOCON 1F
AXIS GALLERY 10月27日（土）〜11月4日（日）　東京都港区六本木5-17-1 Axis Bldg 4F

参加デザイナー
Harri Koskinen, Lustwear, Ilkka Suppanen, Naoto Niidome,
Syrup Helsinki, Pentagon Design, Company

www.lisn.co.jp

Finland Café 2007 soon opened at Jiyugaoka
Finland Café 2007 自由が丘

The 6th Finland Café will soon start. The venue this year is between Jiyugaoka and Denenchofu, along with Kanpachi. By the way, Finland Café is limited period promotional Café, organized by Finnish Tourist Board (MEK). Visitor can enjoy Finnish drinks, foods, interiors, musics, tableware including cutlery with Finnish scenery projected on the wall. The main theme of this year is Finnish Nature (LUONTO). You will experience virtual trip to Finland and enjoy a lot of LUONTO events.

2002年〜2003年は代官山、2004年〜2005年は中目黒、2006年は赤坂と場所を移してきたフィンランド・カフェ、通称"フィンカフェ"。今年は東急東横線「自由が丘」と「田園調布」を最寄駅とする環八沿い、玉川田園調布にオープンする。

フィンランド・カフェとはフィンランド政府観光局（MEK）が主催する期間限定カフェで、店内にはフィンランドのビジュアルが映し出され、フィンランド・ミュージックが流れ、もちろんフィニッシュ・デザインの椅子に座り、イッタラの食器とカトラリーでラピンクルタ（フィンランドのビール）やロバーツコーヒー（フィンランドのカフェ・チェーン）を飲みながら、料理も楽しむことができる。今年のフィンランド・カフェでは"自然（Luonto）"をメインテーマに企画が進行中。店内デコレーションはもちろん、自然に関連したセミナー等も開催する予定。

Finland Café information
Period: 1st Oct - 3rd Nov 2007
Opening hour
Tue, Wed, Thu: 11:00-21:00
Fri, Sat, Sun and national holidays: 11:00-23:00
except for 3rd Nov till 18:00
Mondays closed except for 1st and 8th Oct
Address: 2-7-5 Tamagawa Denenchofu, Setagaya-ku, Tokyo
Telephone: 03 3501 5207
Organizer: Finnish Tourist Board (MEK)
Supported by The Embassy of Finland

期間：10月1日（月）〜11月3日（土）
開店時間：
火、水、木：11:00〜21:00
金、土、日、祝：11:00〜23:00　※11月3日は18:00終了
月定休　※10月1日、10月8日は除く
住所：東京都世田谷区玉川田園調布2-7-5
TEL：03 3501 5207（フィンランド政府観光局）
主催：フィンランド政府観光局（MEK）
後援：フィンランド大使館

www.finlandcafe.com

HOLLAND

Plus Eighty One Voyage
World Travel Information

Lute Suites

Lute Suites is the oft-mentioned designer hotel that was produced by Marcel Wanders, the figurehead of young Dutch designers. The hotel, which was built by renovating the old lodging house of an 18th century gunpowder factory on the outskirts of Amsterdam, features an extravagant set up featuring only seven rooms, all of which are suites. Each of the suites has its own entryway with a completely independent style, and all of the rooms have been decorated with mosaic tiles. These tiles also change to match the mood of each room, ensuring that they are all brimming with personality. The layout and design of the suites are all different as well, giving those who stay there the appealing ability to choose the room that suits their tastes.

オランダ人若手デザイナーの代表格、Marcel Wandersがプロデュースしたことで話題になったデザイン・ホテルLute Suites。アムステルダム郊外にある18世紀の古い火薬工場宿舎をリノベーションして建てられたこのホテルは、全ての部屋がスウィート・ルームで、その数わずか7室という贅沢な造り。個々の部屋に玄関を設けて徹底した独自感を演出しており、どの部屋にもモザイク・タイルを装飾。そのタイルも部屋に合わせて表情を変化させるなど個性溢れた造りになっている。部屋の構造やデザインもそれぞれ異なっているので、宿泊客の好みに合わせて選べるのが最大の魅力だ。

Lute Suites
Address: Amsteldijk Zuid 54-58, 1184 VD, Ouderkerk a/d Amstel
Telephone: +31(0)20 47 22 462
www.lutesuites.com

profile

Marcel Wanders
Born 1963 in Boxtel, Holland. Joined Droog Design after graduating from the 3D design department of the School of the Arts Arnhem. He is known worldwide for designs incorporating unique ideas like his "Knotted Chair" woven of ropes hardened by resin and his candle-shaped "B.L.O. Lamp", which turns on and off at the touch of a breath.

マルセル・ワンダース
1963年オランダ、ボクステル生まれ。アーネム美術学校の3Dデザイン科を卒業後、ドローグ・デザインに参加。ロープを編んで、樹脂で固めた「Knotted Chair（ノッテッド・チェア）」や、息を吹きかけることで点灯・消灯する蝋台型照明「B.L.O Lamp」など、ユニークなアイデアを駆使したデザインで世界的に注目されている。

Dutch design arrival @100% DESIGN TOKYO 2007

Bathroom Mania!

Studio Laurens van Wieringen

Sander Luske

The international contemporary interior design trade fair "100% Design Tokyo 2007" begins on October 31st. Following in the tradition of last year's fair, Dutch designers and design teams will be visiting Japan, with this year's lineup including noteworthy members such as Sander Luske, a product designer responsible for a succession of warm creations in tableware, Bathroom Mania!, a team who puts out bath goods loaded with ideas, Studio Laurens van Wieringen, who are rightfully proud of their richly conceptual rubber products, and Royal Tichelaar Makkum, Holland's oldest ceramics maker with a history that spans over 400 years. This is a chance to experience the depth of Dutch design in its entirety, from flesh designs that go beyond the realm of imagination to basic yet unique items full of quality design.

10月31日にスタートする、コンテンポラリー・インテリアデザインの国際見本市「100% DESIGN TOKYO 2007」。昨年に引き続き、オランダを代表するデザイナーとデザインチームが来日する。テーブルウェアを始めとした温かみのあるプロダクト・デザインを生み出すSander Luske、アイデア満載のバスグッズを発信するBathroom Mania!、発想豊かなラバー製のプロダクツを誇るStudio Laurens van Wieringen、400年もの歴史を持つオランダ最古の陶磁器メーカーRoyal Tichelaar Makkumなど、そうそうたるメンバーが勢揃い。想像の域を超える斬新なデザインから、ベーシックでありながらも独自でデザイン性の高いものまで、オランダ・デザインの奥深さを身近に感じられるチャンス。

100% Design Tokyo 2007
Date: October 31st to November 4th
Location: the big tent in Meiji Jingu Gaien in Aoyama, Tokyo

100%デザイン東京2007
日程：10月31日〜11月4日
場所：東京・青山 神宮外苑大テント内
www.100percentdesign.jp

Designers
Bathroom Mania!, Hybrids+Fusion, Royal Tichelaar Makkum, Sander Luske, Studio Laurens van Wieringen, Studio Samira Boon, Bookarrest, Studio ePosh, Atelier Arnout Visser, Vlieger&Vandam

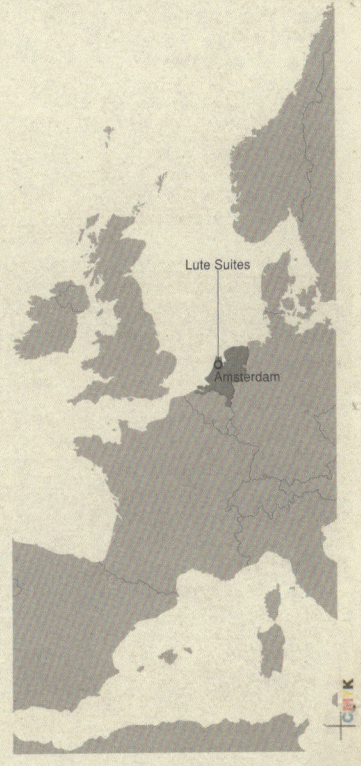

SPAIN

text: Tae Mito from National Tourist Office of Spain

The birth of a modern winery (bodegas) in the southern Basque region of Laguardia
未来的なボデガ（醸造所）が、バスク州南部ラグァルディアに誕生

An odd building with an undulating silver roof, surrounded by the Cordillera Cantabria in a vast vineyard. This is one of the works produced by the architect Santiago Calatrava who was born in Valencia. Bodegas Ysios is arousing attention throughout the world of wine and architecture, for a wine known for the denominacion de origien Rioja, originating from the town of Laguardia, in the Álava district in the Basque region. Moreover, the red wine 'Ysios 2000' was awarded a gold medal in 2004 at the wine fair 'The Japan Wine Challenge' held by the Japan Sommelier Association and the Wine Magazine.

カンタブリア山脈に囲まれた広大なブドウ畑のなかに、波打つ銀色の屋根を持つ奇異な建物。これこそがバレンシア生まれの建築家サンティアゴ・カラトラバが生んだ作品。リオハの原産地呼称を持つワインで知られるバスク州アラバ県の町ラグァルディアに誕生したこのBODEGAS YSIOS（ボデガス・イシオス）が、建築・ワイン業界で話題を呼んでいる。このボデガの赤ワイン「イシオス2000」は、ワイン雑誌と日本ソムリエ協会が開催するワインの品評会「The Japan Wine Challenge」で2004年に金メダルを受賞。

BODEGAS YSIOS
www.bodegasysios.com

Access: 20 minutes by bus to Logrono from Laguardia. (nine buses per day)

アクセス：ログローニョから
ラグァルディアへバスで20分（1日9本）

profile

Santiago Calatrava

The architect Santiago Calatrava was born in Valencia, Spain in 1951. He makes full use of cutting edge constructions, and takes pride in his overwhelmingly beautiful architectural work. Recently in 2004, he handled the Athens Olympic main stadium, and presently, he is said to be the world's leading architect.

サンティアゴ・カラトラバ
1951年スペイン、ヴァレンシア生まれの建築家。最先端の構造を駆使し、圧倒的な建築美を誇る。近年では2004年のアテネオリンピックのメイン・スタジアムを手がけ、現在、世界一の建築家とも言われている。

The origin of an Opera House at 'City of Science and the Arts' in Valencia
バレンシアの「芸術科学都市」に歌劇場誕生

It goes 2 km along the green belt from the inner city area of Valencia, there is complex of Modern architecture 'City of Science and the Arts' what is venturing it by Santiago Calatrava. Here is the newly added Palau de Les Artes Reina Sofía (Queen Sofía Art Gallery). An impressionable opera house on the water's edge, looks like a swan, and also like a enormous fish swallows a ship, depending on the angle. The opening of the opera season this year is the deeply intimate Spanish film director Carlos Saura's stage production of Bizet's 'Carmen' even in Japan. Don't miss the performance of the musical production by the great conductor Lorin Maazel.

バレンシア市街地から緑地帯沿いに2km行くと、サンティアゴ・カラトラバが手がけるの近代建築群「芸術科学都市」が広がる。そこに新たに加わったのがソフィア王妃芸術館（Palau de Les Artes Reina Sofía）。角度によっては、船を飲み込んだ巨大魚のようにも、白鳥のようにも見える、印象的な水辺の歌劇場。今年のオペラシーズンのオープニングは、日本でも馴染み深いスペイン人映画監督カルロス・サウラが舞台演出を担当するビゼーの「カルメン」。偉大な指揮者ロリン・マゼールを音楽監督に迎えての演奏は見逃せない。

Palau de les Arts Reina Sofia
www.lesarts.com

Queen Sofia Art Gallery
Location: Inner city Valencia
Access: 15 minutes walk from Alameda subway station

場所：バレンシア市内
アクセス：地下鉄アラメダ駅から徒歩15分

GERMANY

Deutsche Brunnen Einheitswasserflasche, Günter Kupetz, 1969 ©Informationszentrale Deutsches Mineralwasser (IDM)

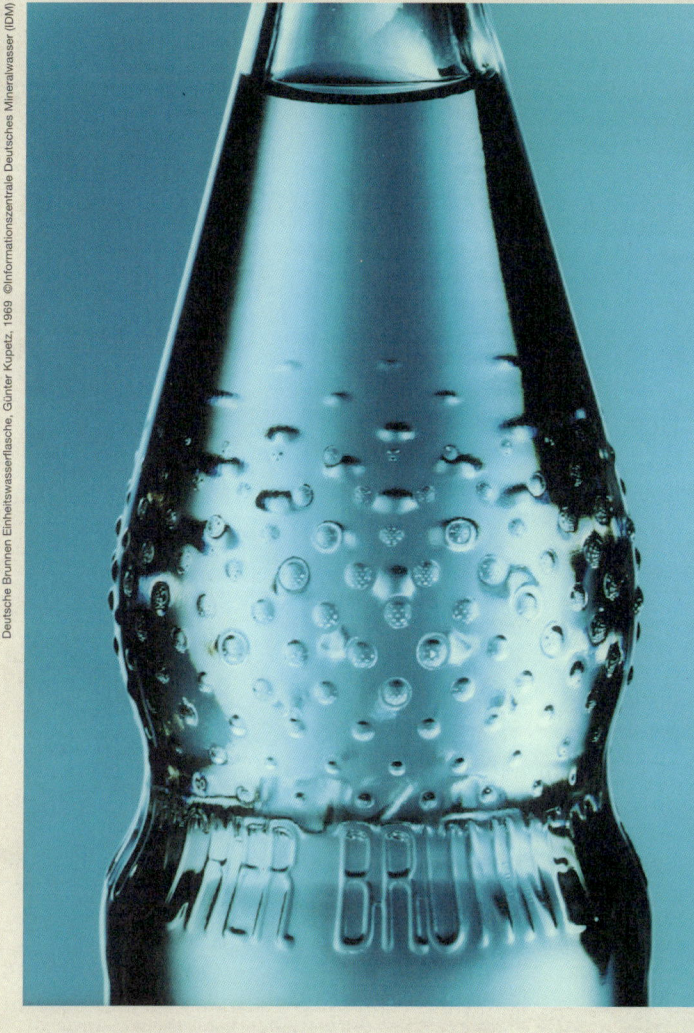

A long-time selling product that shaped German design

ドイツ・デザインを形成するロングセラー商品

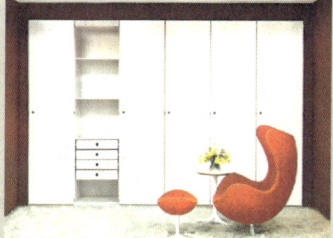

Schranksystem SL, Interlübke, Rolf Heide, 1961
©Gebr. Lübke GmbH & Co. KG

Few German product designs are known for openly showing passion or emotion. If there are any that do this, it would be those that emphasize their power, or functionality and one of them is the famous Porsche 911. The car has barely changed its form over the last 40 years, and other long-time selling products also form the image of German design. Clear-cut designs such as the mineral water bottle by Gunter Kupetz and Interlubke's shelf systems by Rolf Heide are still very much alive today. Many of these long-time selling products have shaped German design.

ドイツのプロダクト・デザインはこれまで、感情を前面に押し出すものはほとんどないと思われがちだ。あるとすれば名車として知られるポルシェ911のように馬力、すなわち性能を重視した製品だけ。そのフォルムは今日まで40年以上も大きく変わることなく生き続けてきたが、他にもドイツ・デザインのイメージとなっているロングセラー商品がある。ギュンター・クペッツのミネラルウォーターのボトル（1969）や、ロルフ・ハイデのインターリュブケ社システム・シェルフSL（1963）など、明確なデザインは今日でも新鮮だ。これら多くのロングセラー商品がドイツ・デザインを形成しているのである。

参照文章：アンドレイ・クペッツ
Reference Text：Andrej kupetz

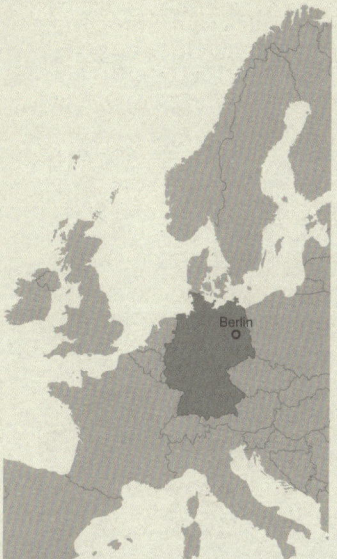

Leica: the compact camera born in Germany

ドイツが生んだ小型カメラ、ライカ

Leica D-Lux, Achim Heine, 2003 ©Leica Camera AG

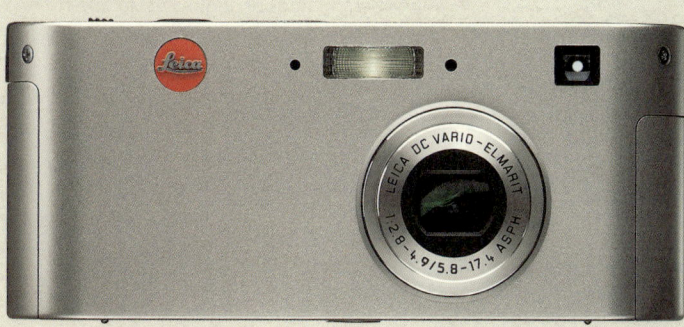

The origin of Leica goes back to 1914 when the head of development Oskar Barnak made the world's first small-film adapted camera, "Ur Leica" by using an exposure checking device for a cinema film. Its well-defined functional beauty and distinctively simple design have added excitement to the world of camera history and is still admired by many. This Leica D-lux is modularly designed by the Berlin designer Achim Heine. With a square body made of surface-treated aluminum for a non-slip hold and clear geometrical form, the camera gives a compact impression.

誕生は1914年、当時、開発責任者であったオスカー・バルナックは映画フィルムの露出をチェックするための器具から、小型フィルムを採用したカメラとしては世界初の成功例とされる「ウル・ライカ」を開発したことに始まる。その研ぎ澄まされた機能美や一目でライカとわかるシンプルなデザインは、世界のカメラ史を彩り、現在も多くの人々を魅了している。今回は、ライカ D-Luxを紹介。モジュール・デザインはベルリンのデザイナー、アヒム・ハイネによるもの。プラスチックにかえ、手から滑り落ちないよう表面加工をしたアルミ製の四角いボディに、明白で幾何学的なフォルムはすっきりとした印象を与えている。

Tea set designed by a master of modern architecture

近代建築の巨匠がデザインしたティーサービス・セット

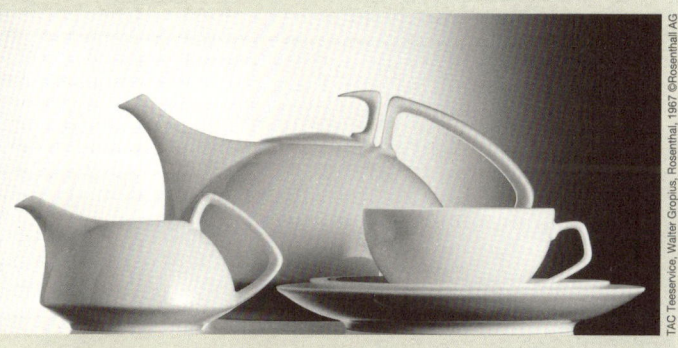

TAC Teeservice, Walter Gropius, Rosenthal, 1967 ©Rosenthal AG

This tea set is from the German's renowned pottery, "Roesenthal". It was designed by the architect Walter Gropius who founded "Bauhaus", a school for design education at Weimer in 1919. The lustrous porcelain surface creates a calm and serene impression. The lid has an upside down L-shape handle so the lid can be pressed down while holding the pot. The white creamer has an identical shape to the tea pot. The hemisphere-shaped cup and round saucer are simple and rather uncharacteristic. With decorative ornamentation stripped away, the tea set possesses a completely different quality from the work of a prestigious pottery that makes luxurious products for royal households. While maintaining its long traditions, this work of creativity and sophistication has adapted to the trends of the times.

ドイツの名窯「ローゼンタール」のティーサービス・セットは、1919年ワイマールに開設された教育機関「バウハウス」の創始者であり建築家のヴァルター・グローピウスによるもの。つやのある白の磁面が、落ち着いた印象を醸し出す。ティーポットは、ポットを持つときに蓋を押さえられるよう、L字を逆さにしたつまみが付いている。ティーポットと同じ形の白いミルクジャグや、半球の形をしたティーカップ、円形のソーサーなど。華美な装飾を限界まで削ぎ落とし、王侯貴族の豪華な名窯とは性質が異る。由緒ある歴史を踏まえながらも、時代に即した創造性豊かで洗練された作品となっている。

www.goethe.de/designtrends

The History of South Africa

It is said that South Africa was originally populated by the Koi people who were herders (Hottentot), and the San people who were a race of hunters (Bushman). Initially there were Southern African people and many sculptures and cave drawings dating from the prehistoric era remain. During the years 300 to 900 A.D, various races of Bantu people, who lived in the north, went southwards, passing through and colonizing all areas. In 1487, the Portuguese national Bartolomeu Dias discovered the Cape of Good Hope at the southern tip of South Africa and in 1497 Portuguese national Vasco da Gama discovered Natal. Europeans began immigrating into settlements created in Cape Town, in 1652, by the Dutch national Jan van Riebeeck, as a relay base for trade in the East Orient for the Dutch East India Company. Immigrants from Holland, named these developing new settlements Boer, meaning farmer in the Afrikaans and Dutch. In addition, in the 17th century, a large number of the French national Huguenot who fled to Holland immigrated. The addition of new immigrants to the colony and the expansion towards inland, brought about a clash with the Xhosa tribe, who are one of the African Bantu tribes, and their land was taken.
In 1795, the British who had a powerful military force, recognized the key position of the Indian sea route from the Cape of Good Hope, and seized the sovereignty of the colony on the cape from the Dutch. Consequently, the influence from the Britain intensified; for instance, English became the official language, and the British judicial system came into use. The Boer people who could not comprehend English, were discriminated against and began to call themselves Afrikaner. Afrikaners moved further apart towards inland areas, and founded Orange self-governing county, and the Republic of Transvaal. Then in 1867, diamonds were discovered in Orange self-governing county, and in 1886, gold ore was discovered in the Republic of Transvaal. This was the motive for the outbreak of the Boer wars (South African War) over sovereignty of the gold producing areas, occurring twice, between the Afrikaners and the British. The British won the war in 1910, and combined 4 states and established the Union of South Africa of dominion. Afrikaners brought about a new state, together with stressing the right for a greater awareness of nationalism, and enacted one law after another distinguishing between the rights for each race. The political power, the Nationalist Party established itself in 1948, and implemented the policy of apartheid. However, this policy received criticism from international societies, and in 1961, the country named The Republic of South Africa broke away from the British Commonwealth.
In 1976, the Soweto uprising began, and during the 1980's antiestablishment movement became violent, and anti-apartheid campaigning grew with the implementation of international economic sanctions. Frederik Willem de Klerk who was inaugurated as president in 1989, moved forward with the abolition of apartheid, and in 1990 the former chairman of the African National Congress, Nelson Mandela, was released after a life of 27 years in prison, and in the following year, all political prisoners were released. In the 1990's, a decision was reached to finally repeal laws relating to apartheid, and to abolish all racially discriminating laws. In 1994 the political power, the African National Congress, participated in an all-race general election for the first time in history, and Nelson Mandela was inaugurated as president. Thabo Mbeki of the ANC was inaugurated as vice-president, and Frederik Willem de Klerk, the previous president, and head of the South African Nationalist Party was inaugurated as vice-president. In 1996, a new constitution was adopted that banned all discrimination. In 1999, Thabo Mbeki was elected vice-president in the second general election. Nelson Mandela declared 'My work is done.' and resigned as president after his first term and withdrew from the political world. In 2004, the ruling party, the African National Congress, with over 70 percent of the votes, won a landslide victory for the third time in as many general elections.

南アフリカの歴史

南アフリカにはもともと、狩猟民族のサン人（ブッシュマン）と牧畜民族のコイ人（ホッテントット）が住んでいたといわれている。初期の南部アフリカ人であり、先史時代からの石窟画や彫刻を多く残している。300～900年代には、北方に住んでいたバンツー系の諸民族が南下し、全域に渡って定着した。1487年に、ポルトガルのバルトロメウ・ディアス(Bartolomeu Dias)が南アフリカ南端の喜望峰を発見し、1497年にポルトガルのヴァスコ・ダ・ガマ(Vasco da Gama)がナタールを発見。1652年にオランダ人のヤン・ファン・リーベック(Jan van Riebeeck)がオランダ東インド会社の東洋貿易の中継基地として、ケープタウンに居留地を作ったのがヨーロッパ人の入植のはじまり。オランダからの移民は、自らをボーア(オランダ語及びアフリカーンス語で農民の意)と称して入植地を開拓していった。また、17世紀にはオランダに亡命していたフランス人のユグノー(新教徒)も多数移住。入植者の増加で植民地は内陸に向けて拡大し、バンツー系アフリカ人の一部族であるコーサ族との衝突が起こり、その度に土地が奪われていた。
1795年、強大な軍事力を持っていたイギリスは、喜望峰をインド航路の重要拠点と認識し、オランダからケープ植民地の支配権を奪取する。その後英語が公用語になり、イギリスの司法制度が用いられるなど、イギリスの影響が強まる。英語を解さないボーア人は差別を受け、自らをアフリカーナーと呼ぶようになる。アフリカーナーはケープを離れて内陸部へと移動し、トランスバール共和国やオレンジ自治国を建国。その後1867年にオレンジ自治国でダイヤモンドが、1886年にはトランスバール共和国で金鉱が発見される。それをきっかけに、イギリスとアフリカーナーとの間に2回にわたる、金の産地支配権を巡ったボーア戦争（南アフリカ戦争）が勃発する。戦争はイギリスが勝利し、1910年にアフリカーナーの4州を統合して、自治領の南アフリカ連邦(Union of South Africa)を設立する。アフリカーナーは新国家誕生とともに民族主義意識を強めて権利を主張し、人種ごとに権利を区別する法律を次々と制定した。1948年に政権を樹立した国民党は、アパルトヘイト（人種隔離）政策を実施したが、国際社会から非難され、1961年に英連邦から脱退して国名を「南アフリカ共和国」とする。
1976年のソウェト蜂起にはじまり、1980年代にかけて反体制運動は激しくなり、国際的に経済制裁を受け、反アパルトヘイト運動が高まる。1989年に大統領に就任したフレデリック・ウィレム・デクラーク(Frederik Willem de Klerk)は、アパルトヘイト廃止を推し進め、1990年にアフリカ民族会議の元議長ネルソン・マンデラを27年半という獄中生活から釈放し、翌91年には全政治犯を釈放した。1990年代に入ってようやくアパルトヘイト関連法の撤廃、人種差別法の法律全廃を決定した。1994年に行われた史上初の全人種が参加した総選挙によりANC(アフリカ民族会議)が政権をとり、ネルソン・マンデラ(Nelson Mandela)が大統領に就任。副大統領に、ANCのタボ・ムベキ(Thabo Mbeki)と国民党党首のフレデリック・ウィレム・デクラーク前大統領が就任。1996年にはあらゆる差別を禁止した新憲法が採択された。1999年、第2回総選挙でタボ・ムベキ副大統領が当選。ネルソン・マンデラは「私の仕事は終わった。」と言って一期で大統領を辞め、政界から引退した。2004年の3度目となる総選挙でも与党ANCが70%を超える得票率で圧勝。タボ・ムベキ大統領が再選され、現在に至る。

Dreamy voyage through South African design
夢の南アフリカ・デザインの旅

Kruger Safari

Everybody wants to experience the dream of seeing wild animals amongst the vast nature of African savannas and jungles at least once. The world's largest scale natural park, the Kruger National Park, approximately 20,000 square kilometers, with 147 kinds of mammals, and 500 kinds of birds, is a treasure trove of wild animals. A park of continuous savannas and forests of low trees and bushes, where it is possible to see the activities of wild animals close up. The Kruger Park is located approximately 5 hours (500 kilometers) by car from Johannesburg, neighboring Mozambique and Zimbabwe.

アフリカのジャングルやサバンナで野生の動物を見ることは、誰もが一度は経験したい夢のひとつである。世界最大級の自然公園、クルーガー・ナショナル・パーク（Kuruger National Park）は、約2万平方キロに147種の哺乳類と500種の鳥類がいる野生動物の宝庫である。低木林とサバンナの続く公園では、野生の動物の営みを間近で見ることができる。クルーガー国立公園は、ジンバブエ、モザンビークに隣接しヨハネスブルグから、車で約5時間（500km）ほどの位置にある。

▲ キャンプ場では、ほとんどのものが揃っており、思い思いにアフリカサバンナを楽しむことができる。欧米のリピーターが多く、ゆっくりと時間をかけてアフリカの醍醐味を満喫している。おすすめは1週間程度滞在して、北のキャンプ場から、南のキャンプ場までベースキャンプを移動しながら、地形や生息動物の変化を楽しむ方法である。アフリカサファリは、誰もが手軽に経験できるので、旅行の選択肢に加えてみてはいかがだろう。その体験は一生の思い出に残るはずである。

サファリ用語で"ゲーム"という言葉がよく使われる。一度サファリを体験するとその言葉の意味が分かる。動物が活発に動く時間は、夜明けと日が沈む夕刻に絞られる。野生の動物は、常に動いているので、どこにいけば会えるかは分からない。また、目を凝らして探さないと見逃してしまう。早朝の水辺や動物の足跡、フンの新しさなどで目的の動物を探すのだが、突然、予告もなく象やライオンは目の前に現れてくる。動物、鳥類図鑑を片手に出会った動物をひとつずつチェックしていき、未だ出会えない動物を探しに他の場所に車を駆る。1日、朝夕2セットのまさに動物を探しまわるサファリウォッチング・ゲームなのである。そして、ゲーム終了後の昼、夜の過ごし方がサファリに一層の楽しみを与えてくれる。雄大な眺めと木漏れ日で芝生に寝転び過ごす日中や、満天に輝く星に包まれる夜更けの静けさを感じ過ごす時間。都会の喧噪と世俗の悩みに解放され、自然の厳しさと喜びを教えてくれ、生きている実感を与えてくれる。日常生活をしばし忘れ、悠久の大自然に触れてみよう。

▲ 今回のサファリガイドのUDOがコーディネートしてくれたテーブルは、キャンプ場で注目を浴びていた。

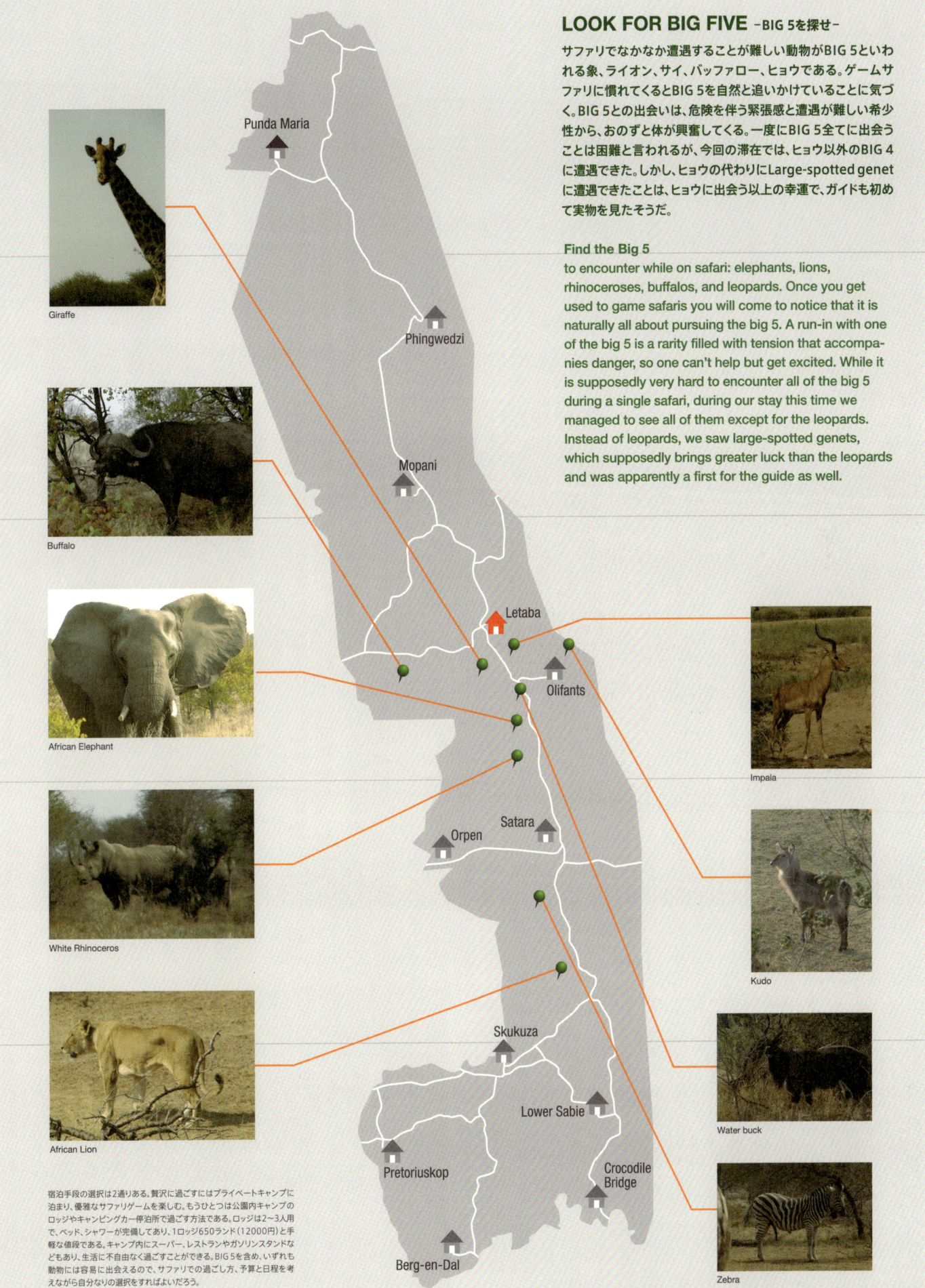

LOOK FOR BIG FIVE －BIG 5を探せ－

サファリでなかなか遭遇することが難しい動物がBIG 5といわれる象、ライオン、サイ、バッファロー、ヒョウである。ゲームサファリに慣れてくるとBIG 5を自然と追いかけていることに気づく。BIG 5との出会いは、危険を伴う緊張感と遭遇が難しい希少性から、おのずと体が興奮してくる。一度にBIG 5全てに出会うことは困難と言われるが、今回の滞在では、ヒョウ以外のBIG 4に遭遇できた。しかし、ヒョウの代わりにLarge-spotted genetに遭遇できたことは、ヒョウに出会う以上の幸運で、ガイドも初めて実物を見たそうだ。

Find the Big 5

to encounter while on safari: elephants, lions, rhinoceroses, buffalos, and leopards. Once you get used to game safaris you will come to notice that it is naturally all about pursuing the big 5. A run-in with one of the big 5 is a rarity filled with tension that accompanies danger, so one can't help but get excited. While it is supposedly very hard to encounter all of the big 5 during a single safari, during our stay this time we managed to see all of them except for the leopards. Instead of leopards, we saw large-spotted genets, which supposedly brings greater luck than the leopards and was apparently a first for the guide as well.

宿泊手段の選択は2通りある。贅沢に過ごすにはプライベートキャンプに泊まり、優雅なサファリゲームを楽しむ。もうひとつは公園内キャンプのロッジやキャンピングカー停泊所で過ごす方法である。ロッジは2～3人用で、ベッド、シャワーが完備してあり、1ロッジ650ランド（12000円）と手軽な値段である。キャンプ内にスーパー、レストランやガソリンスタンドなどもあり、生活に不自由なく過ごすことができる。BIG 5を含め、いずれも動物には容易に出会えるので、サファリでの過ごし方、予算と日程を考えながら自分なりの選択をすればよいだろう。

▲ **A waterside paradise**
At the water's edge, many animals and birds gather fleetingly surrounded by peaceful scenery.
水辺の楽園。多くの動物や鳥が集まる、つかの間の平和の風景。

Kruger Safari

▲ Wild kingdom
Herds of elephants and contrasting nature of this magnificent African wild kingdom speak volumes.
野生の王国。象の群れと自然の対比がアフリカの雄大さを物語る。

▲ Ravenous lions attacking impala. The force of sprinting lions, a scene only from the wild.
インパラに襲いかかる飢えたライオン。疾走するライオンの迫力は野生ならではの光景である。

▲ 車の目の前まで飢えたライオンは近づく。

Wilderness Trail
-Walking SAFARI-

A walking game where one follows the footprints of wild animals on foot, getting out of the car for 4 hours in a savanna.

This is a walking safari where one can get out of the jeep and walk around, whilst being guarded by a ranger equipped automatic small arms and a guide with a rifle. You step cautiously on the firm ground of the savanna with the sound of your own footsteps echoing around your mind. Waking a person's senses to wild animals, who are perceptive of all surrounding signs, the tension increases. Here, animals and humans become nothing other than one.

サバンナを4時間走り、車から降りて、自分の足で野生動物の足跡を追いかけるゲーム。
ライフルを持ったガイドと自動小銃を装備したレンジャーに警護されながらジープを降りて歩くのが、ウォーキングサファリである。
サバンナの大地を踏みしめる自分の足音が脳幹まで響き渡る。緊張感が高まり、周囲の気配を全て察知しようとする動物の野生の感覚を人に呼び起こさせる。ここでは人も動物の一種類にすぎない。

▲ 日の出前の水場にいるハイエナ。

▲ 足跡をたどりながら野生の動物を追い続ける。

突然、10m先にしろサイが現れ、緊張感は最高潮に達する。目だけがサイの動きを追い、体は動くことができない金縛り状態である。裸同然の人間にとって野生の動物の全てが脅威である。
自分もサバンナを生きる動物になり、野生との一体感を味わうことができた瞬間だった。アフリカのサバンナを歩く、これほど思い出に残る出来事はないだろう。

▲ Stalling

▲ Hadedah Ibis

▲ Roller

▲ Hornbill

Bird Safari

In the Kruger National Pak, searching for over 500 species of birds is also fun. Bringing along a catalogue of birds obtained from the camp increase the fun.

クルーガー・ナショナルパークでは、500種類を超える鳥類を探すのも楽しみである。キャンプで手に入る鳥類カタログをもっていけば楽しさも倍増する。

▲ Crowned Lapwing

▲ Buzzard

▲ Heron

▲ Crested Barbet

▲走るごとに周囲は赤く染まっていく。

▲道路脇まで火が燃え広がっている。

▲火災の状況を調査する山林警備隊。

▲近郊の村にも影響はでているが、慣れているせいか、普段のままの生活である。

Forest fire

Encounter mountain fires burning continuously for three days. Mountain fires are not rare in this dry area of the Kruger region, but we were surprised by the huge scale of smoke. For humans, no technology can surpass such nature.

3日間燃え続ける山火事に遭遇。乾燥地帯であるクルーガー地域では、山火事は珍しいことではないらしいが、その巨大な煙のスケールにも驚かされる。人間ではなすすべも無い自然の脅威である。

ヨハネスブルグからクルーガーまでの道のりは、ただひたすらに真直ぐの道が続く。
途中、村々で休憩しながらアフリカの壮大な景色を眺め走る、ロードムービーのような旅を満喫できる。

Along the way

ヨハネスブルグからクルーガーまでの道のりは、ただひたすらに真直ぐの道が続く。
途中、村々で休憩しながらアフリカの壮大な景色を眺め走る、ロードムービーのような旅を満喫できる。

▲ Bourke's Luck Potholes（ブライデ・リバー・キャニオン自然保護区内）
Treur River（悲しみの川）と Blade River（喜びの川）が滝壺で混ざり
合い、小さな渦を巻き一体となる伝説物語の観光名所。入場料20R。

Blyde River Canyon Natuer Reserve

The majestic gorge, in the nature reserve, which borders on to the Kruger National Park. This is a spot, that you will want to stop to take a break, on the way to the Kruger National Park.

ブライデ・リバー・キャニオン自然保護区
クルーガー国立公園に隣接する雄大な渓谷が続く自然保護区。
クルーガー国立公園に行く途中に休憩も兼ねて立ち寄りたいスポット。

Cape Town

If you draw your finger around the globe, the last place you will reach is Cape Town, the southernmost located city in the world. As its name suggests, Cape Town is located on a cape peninsula surrounded by the Atlantic Ocean to the west and the Indian Ocean to the east. The Cape of Good Hope, the southernmost point of Africa, divides these two oceans.

In this Wine Land full of fertile soil an air of colonial elegance drifts about, and from the center of the peninsula Table Mountain, spiritual heart of this land, stands proudly. Beautiful oceans, gorgeous mountains, rich earth; all the blessings of nature can be found here.

The lifestyle of Cape Town brings new pleasures and fulfillment to adults who have both splendor and grace. Magnificent and refined. There is no other city that is more suited to these words than Cape Town.

地球儀を指でなぞると最後に辿り着く、最南端の都市ケープタウン。
西が大西洋に、東がインド洋に囲まれたケープ半島。
アフリカ最南の地"喜望峰"は、そのふたつの海を分岐する。

肥沃な大地が広がるワインランドには、コロニアル時代の優雅さが
漂い、半島の中央には心の故郷テーブルマウンテンが屹立する。
美しい海や山、肥沃な大地とあらゆる自然の恵みを享受する。

ケープタウンのライフスタイルは、華麗さと優雅さを兼ね備えた、
大人の人生に、新たな喜びと満足を与えてくれる。
華麗に優雅。この言葉が最も似合う都市、それがケープタウン。

Table Mountain

In West Cape state, the summit of this flat mountain appears as if it has been cut with a knife. It has been named from its shape, which looks like a table. Looking up at the figure of the mountain from Cape Town has become a symbol of this town, and the clouds and mist which shroud the summit, has been called 'Tablecloth' by local people. A cable car service runs to the summit and there are several hiking routes, and the panoramic view of the city of Cape Town from the summit is magnificent. The mountain is one of the leading sightseeing spot for tourists who visit to Cape Town.

西ケープ州にある、頂上がナイフで切られたかのように平らになっている山。テーブルのような形からこの名前が付けられた。ケープタウンから見上げたその姿は街の象徴となっており、頂上にかかっている雲や霧は、現地の人々に「テーブルクロス」と呼ばれている。山頂へはケーブルカーが運行されているほか、複数のハイキングルートがあり、そこから一望できるケープタウン市街は絶景。この地を訪れる旅行者の代表的な観光スポットのひとつとなっている。

▲ テーブルマウンテンの頂上よりの眺め。

Cape Grace Hotel

This five star hotel is a symbol of Cape Town. This is the Cape Grace Hotel. This hotel was built ten years ago, and people from the world of business and well-known people from all over the world continue to love its high quality service and elegance. This hotel provides the highest quality service in all areas, from the individual lobby front style, the library, to its spa. Its popularity is such that more than half of the guests, who stay here, come back again. Expansive rooms with spacious en-suite bathrooms, providing a pleasant way to wake up. Looking up out of the window, one can see Table Mountain and below, one will see the yacht harbor, with a view of Atlantic Ocean. You will know the meaning of the symbol of Cape Town when you gaze upon the exterior of this hotel. The Cape Grace Hotel, with the scenery of Table Mountain, the landmark of Cape Town, reflects an elegant silhouette, and a beauty that will make you gasp for breath. This is a hotel that will make guests enjoy the most lavish and elegant perfection. This is the Cape Grace Hotel.

ケープ・グレース・ホテル

ケープタウンを象徴する5星ホテル。その名も"Cape Grace Hotel"。この地に建てられ10年経ったばかりだが、上質なサービスとその優雅さで、世界中の著名人、政財界人から愛され続けている。個別デスクのフロント・スタイルから、ライブラリー、スパとあらゆる面で、最高の上質なサービスを提供するために造られたホテル。宿泊者の半数以上がリピーター客という人気である。ゆったりした客室の広さとバスルームは、旅の目覚めを快適にさせる。部屋の窓を見上げれば、テーブルマウンテンが姿を現し、見下ろせばヨットハーバー越しに大西洋を臨む。ホテル外観からも、ケープタウンを象徴するホテルという意味が分かるだろう。Cape Grace Hotelは、ケープタウンのランドマーク、テーブルマウンテンを背景に息をのむほどの美しさで、優雅なシルエットを映しだす。最高の贅沢と優雅さを享受させる成熟した大人のためのホテル。それがCape Grace Hotelである。

Cape Grace Hotel
West Quay V&A Waterfront
Cape Town South Africa
Tel : +27 21 410 7100
Fax : +27 21 419 7622
www.capegrace.com

Cape of Good Hope

The cape was discovered by the Portuguese national, Bartolomeu Dias in 1488. It is easy to think of the Cape of Good Hope as South Africa's southernmost tip, however, it is Cape Agulhas, which is located 150 kilometers from the Cape of Good Hope. The southern part of the Cape Peninsula is a nature reserve, which is inhabited by more than 150 species of animals, such as ostriches, baboons, zebras, and mongoose, and one can also see local flowers, such as, Fine Bush, and Protea. In addition, it is also known for the meeting point between the two seas; the Indian Ocean and the Atlantic Ocean.

1488年、ポルトガル人のバルトロメウ・ディアス（Bartolomeu Dias）によって発見された岬。アフリカの最南端と思われがちだが、実際はここから約150kmのアガラス岬（アグラス岬）が最南端に位置する。半島南部が喜望峰自然保護区となっており、ダチョウ、ヒヒ、シマウマ、マングースなど150種類以上の動物が生息しているほか、プロテアやフィンボスなどの花が見られる。また、インド洋と大西洋の2つの海が出会う場所としても知られている。

1.2.3.4.
Cape of Good Hope

▲ Cape point

1.

2.

3.

4.

▲ ケープポイントから喜望峰を望む。

Cape Point

▲ 大西洋とインド洋の海流が交わる。

037

▲ Mist shore

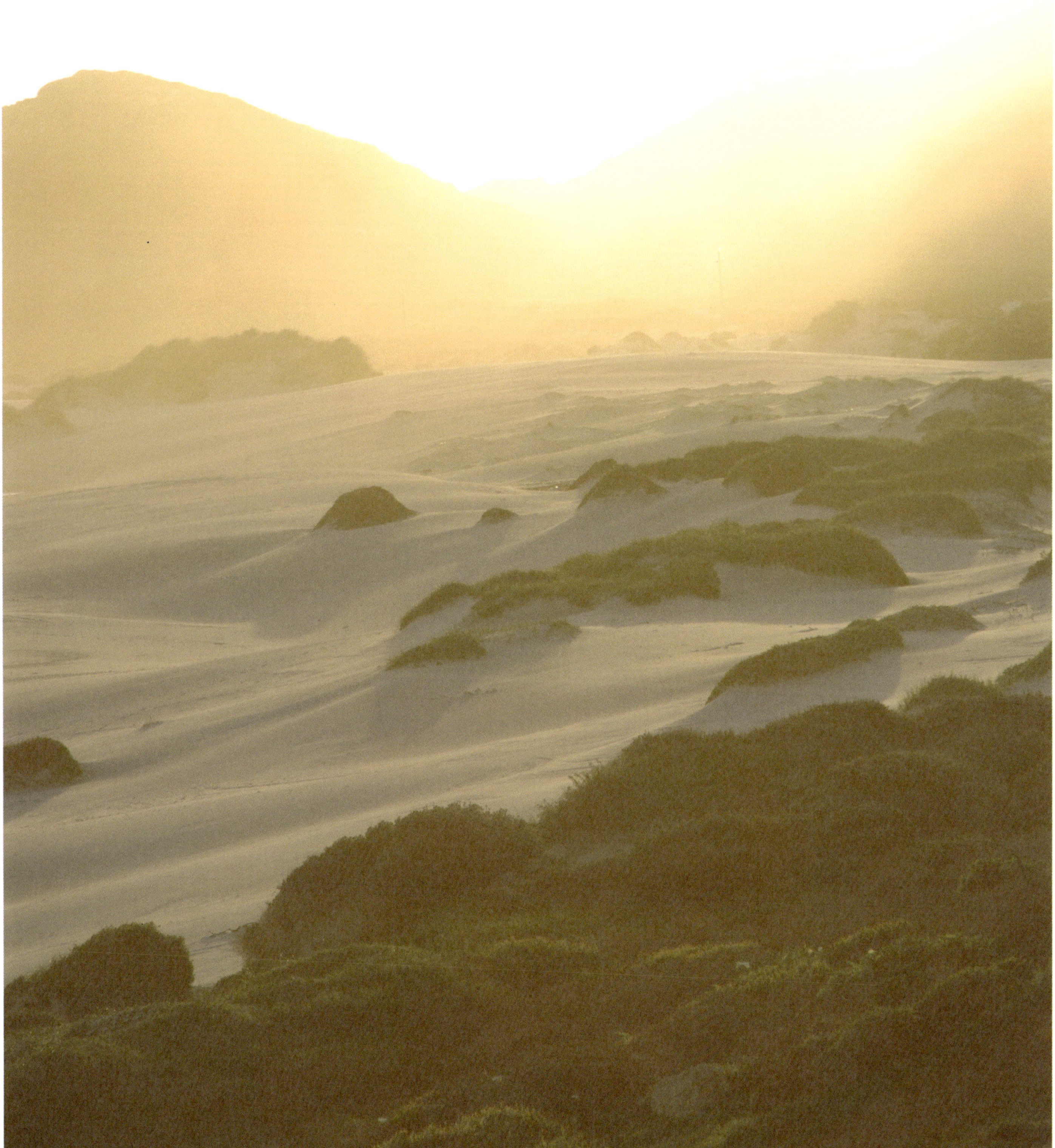

Boulders Beach

Many Humboldt penguins inhabit the surrounding areas of Cape Town, and are known as Cape Penguins. The penguins are approximately 70 cm tall, black and white, with a black area around their chests. They lay eggs all year round, but the peak period is between February and May, and November to December. The hatching baby penguins spend the first year in the sea, and in the molting season they return to their original breeding place. On the east coast of Cape Town is Boulders beach, and here it is possible to see groups of penguins all year round in the shore and coastal thickets. During the twentieth century the number of inhabitants have dramatically decreased resulting from petroleum and crude oil sea pollution spilling from sinking tankers close to the breading ground, causing the death of several hundred thousand penguins.

ボルダーズ・ビーチ
フンボルトペンギンに属するペンギンで、ケープタウン周辺に多く生息するため「ケープペンギン」と呼ばれている。体調は約70cm、胸に黒い帯のような模様があり、白と黒のツートンカラー。産卵は1年中行われるが、2〜5月と11〜12月がピーク期で、孵化したヒナは、最初の1年を海で過ごし、換羽期に繁殖地へ戻ってくる。ケープタウン東岸にあるボルダーズ・ビーチでは、海岸とその手前にある茂みでこのペンギンの群れを年中見る事ができる。20世紀に入ってから、繁殖地の近くで沈没したタンカーから流出した石油や原油の海洋汚染により、数10万羽のケープペンギンが死に追いやられたため、生息数が急激に減少している。

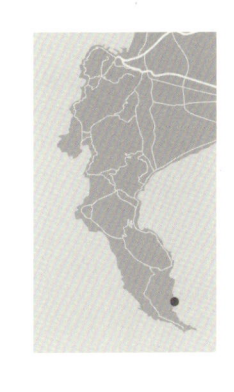

Cape Town

Table bay faces the Republic of South Africa's second city. The capital's legislative branch of the government is in the state capital of West Cape. In 1952, a town was established as a relay base for trade in the orient for the East India Company, which was called Mother City, and this area became the birthplace of South Africa.

In 1994, Nelson Mandela, who was a central figure in the movement to abolish apartheid, became the first black president of the Republic of South Africa, after being imprisoned on Robben Island, far out to sea off shore from Cape Town.

Cape Town spreads out from the foot of the mountains towards the sea, and is becoming South Africa's best sightseeing city. There are plenty of places of interest, such as wineries, the historical world heritage site, Robben Island, Table Mountain and the Cape Peninsula, which represent the area's rich nature.

A_ 2010年のワールドカップのための建設中の競技場。進行が遅れて世界的に話題になっているが、建設は急ピッチで進められている。

B_ Sunday Market：日曜日はダウンタウンの店が休みなので、買い物したい人は訪れてみては。

C_ Ambassader Hotel：Bentry Beachに面した4星ホテル。今回3日間宿泊したホテルで、部屋からのオーシャンビューは最高である。

D_ Restaurant Salt：Cape Townで、いま最も人気のあるレストラン。金、土の夜はドレスアップしたカップルであふれかえるケープタウン随一のおしゃれスポット。

E_ Lion's Head：テーブルマウンテンとともにケープタウンのシンボル的な山。

AREA 2_ ダウンタウンの路上駐車徴収人：ダウンタウンで駐車すると、すぐにどこからともなく徴収に来る係りの人。駐車時間により、3R（3分／50円）～7R（7時間／120円）支払わないと違反になり罰金を課せられる。また似たような服を着て金を取ろうとする連中も多いので注意しよう。

テーブル湾に面する南アフリカ共和国第2の都市。立法府の首都であり、西ケープ州の州都。1952年に東インド会社の東洋貿易の中継基地として建設された町で、南アフリカ発祥の地として「マザー・シティ」とも呼ばれている。アパルトヘイト廃止運動の中心人物、そして1994年に黒人初の南アフリカ共和国大統領になったネルソン・マンデラ（Nelson Mandela）は、ケープタウン沖合にあるロベン島に幽閉されていた。街は山の裾野から海に向かって広がっており、テーブルマウンテンやケープ半島に代表される豊かな自然、世界遺産であるロベン島などの歴史的なスポット、ワイナリーなど多くの見所があり、南アフリカ随一の観光都市となっている。

AREA 1_ Victoria & Alfred Water Front：レストラン、ショッピング、映画館、ホテルなど全てのものが揃っている最も治安の良いエリア。おしゃれスポット。

F_ Cape Grace Hotel：33Pで紹介した5星ホテル。

昼間は明るく、にぎやかなケープタウンのダウンタウンだが、土日と陽が沈んでからは、決して歩かないようにしたい。交通のアクセスは良いと言えないケープタウンをエンジョイするならレンタカーを借りることだ。車で30分も走ると海やワイン畑の丘陵地に容易に行け、ウォーターフロント地区以外は、身動きできない夜間でも自由に行動することが可能になる。道路の整備は万全で交通マナーも素晴らしく良く、日本と同じ左側通行なので、日本で運転するより運転しやすい。道も複雑ではなく、ダウンタウンなどは、一日走れば、道路を覚えてしまうほど分かりやすい。海外で運転することに臆病になるかも知れないがケープタウンを10倍楽しむためには勇気をだしてみよう。レンタカー料金が日本の半額程度ということも魅力である。

レンタカーの注意点
基本的にはマニュアル車である。オートマ車やCD付きは保険代などで驚くほど高くなる。CDのある車は極端に盗難に狙われやすいからである。ラジオで音楽は十分楽しめるので必要はないだろう。ガソリン代は日本とそれほど変わらないと考えたほうがよい。空港からケープタウン市内までのタクシー料金で、小型車を一日借りれる。道路も分かりやすく、喜望峰やテーブルマウンテンへも自分たちで運転して行けるので、かなりの利便性がある。海沿いの細い道や町中の駐車などを考慮すると小型車を借りることをおすすめする。

夜間の行動
昼間の安全なケープタウンに比べると夜の行動は十分気をつけるべきだ。ウォータフロント地区以外は出歩かないほうが賢明である。とは言ってもせっかく旅をしに来たのに外に出れないのも寂しい。ズール音楽を聴きながら、食事ができる手頃なレストランもダウンタウンには数多くある。旅の思い出に訪れてみよう。いま、世界で話題のズールラップのメッカがケープタウンである。タウンガイド誌を手に入れれば情報は手に入るので、気になる店を調べ、車で行ってみよう。
基本的に町中でも特定場所以外はどこでも駐車できるので、行き先の店を調べ、店の前に駐車して遊びに行く。歩く距離を最低限度にするのだ。タクシーで帰る際には、必ず店で呼んでもらうこと。ヨーロッパやアメリカで旅慣れた人こそ注意してほしい。美しい街といえどここは、アフリカ。大酒を飲んで騒いでいる留学生がよく襲われるという話を聞いた。潰れるほど飲むことは危険この上ないことを認識しよう。もちろん運転者が酒を飲むことは論外である。

M_ Safety Drive：事故も多いので、安全運転に注意。

K_ South Africa National Gallery：南アフリカ国立美術館

L_ THE OLD BISCUIT MILL：Wood Stockにあるショッピングモール。小さいながらユニークなショップと独特の雰囲気のモール。おしゃれスポット。

G_ Salsa Club：おしゃれ黒人が集まるレストランクラブ。道路沿いにあり、目立つので分かりやすい。

H_ The Africa Café：アフリカン料理を食べられる人気のレストラン。

I_ Zula Bar：ズール音楽や、ズールラップなどが聴けるレストランバー。

J_ Cape Town Station：市内唯一の鉄道列車の終着駅。遠方からの人たちのたまり場にもなっており、危険地域なので近づかないほうが良い。

043

People

Elegance and Grace

Wine Land

Restaurant

Franschoek

One of the Wine Lands on the outskirts of Cape Town. Its name originates as a word meaning French district. The district is famous for its many delicious restaurants and is known as the Cape's gourmet area. If you have to pick just one eatery to visit on a daytrip to Franshoek, apparently the place to choose is Le Petete Ferme. As the restaurant is also an auberge (or inn) lodging is also available, so for wine lovers this makes an excellent starting point for any exploration of the area.

Franschoek：フランシュフック地区

ケープタウン郊外のワインランド地域のひとつ。地区名称は、フランス地区の言葉から由来している。この地区は美味しいレストランが多いことでも有名で、ケープ地方のグルメ・エリアとなっている。日帰りで1軒だけ選ぶならば、ここ"La Petete Ferme"と言われている。オーベルジュとして宿泊もできるので、ワイン愛好家ならば、ここを起点に巡るのもよいだろう。

▲ 温野菜のミルフィーユ

▲ 冷製のガスパチョ

Wine

In the Wine Land districts there are several vineyards where visitors can sample five or six different varieties of wine and compare the types of African wine grapes until they find the one that suits their tastes. After the third stop you'll probably have sampled quite a bit, so those without a healthy tolerance for alcohol should probably take things in moderation.

ここワインランド地区では、5～6種類のワイン試飲のできるワイン農園が数多くあり、アフリカ・ワインのブドウ品種などを飲み比べながら好みに合ったワインを探すことができる。3軒ほど巡るとかなりの量になるので、お酒の強くない人は、ほどほどに。

▲ ワインランドで南アフリカ・ワインの試飲を楽しむ。

HISTORY OF WINE

The history of South African wine is surprisingly old. Within a few short years from when the Dutch first colonized, in 1652, they made vineyards in the Cape area, and began producing wine in 1659. The vast grape growing region, located on the same southerly latitude of 34 degrees, as Chile, and Australia, extends from Cape Town to Klein Karoo, and they say this area has everything for cultivating grapes; a tranquil Mediterranean kind of climate, and ample daylight hours. Generally, in 1918 the famous wine KWV, established grape cultivating farms as cooperatives, and unique varieties such as Pinotage, and Chenin Blanc, which represent the wines of South Africa, and are wines made from original rich grapes, with a high degree of maturation, that are appreciated all over the world. Now, lets introduce a few of the recommended South African wines.

南アフリカ・ワインの歴史は意外に古く、オランダ人などが入植（1652年）して間もない1659年、ケープ地区にブドウ畑が作られワインが製造された。ケープタウンからクラインカルーまで続く広大なブドウ栽培地域はオーストラリア、チリと同じ南緯34度に位置し、穏やかな地中海性気候や豊富な日照時間など、ブドウ栽培に適した全てがあると言われている。一般的に1918年にブドウ栽培農家が協同組合として設立したKWVのワインが有名で、南アフリカを代表する独特の品種ピノタージュや白のシュナン・ブランなど、成熟度の高い個性豊かなブドウから生まれるワインは世界各地で愛飲されている。ここでは、おすすめの南アフリカ・ワインを紹介しよう。

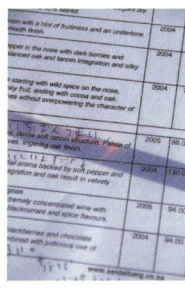

1. 2. 3. 4.

1. Chenin Blanc
With a transparent pale barley color, the nuance of the fragrances of Chinese quince and melon, imbibe and you will think of lime, a slight acidity, and a rich fruitiness, as you swallow.

2. Pinotage
A deep dark ruby color, a rich fruity fragrance, a complex flavor produced from a mature barrel, and a flavor becoming sturdy and strong.

3. Cathedral Cellar Cabernet Sauvignon
A deep dark reddish purple colored wine, with a complex taste originating from the use of a mature barrel, and a condensed fruitiness, that is its characteristic. This is a well-balanced wine, which can be enjoyed in its youth.

4. Roodeberg
A fresh and bold berry-like aroma unfurls, followed by a spiciness that comes from maturing in casks. The taste is smooth, with a deft strength.

1. シュナン・ブラン
透明がかった淡い麦わら色、カリンとメロンのニュアンスのある香り、口に含むとライムを想わせる微かな酸味を豊富な果実味が包みこむ。
色／白／品種：シュナン・ブラン／価格：¥950（税別）

2. ピノタージュ
深く濃いルビー色、果実の香り豊かで、樽熟成によって複雑な風味が生まれ、たくましくコクのある味わいとなっている。
色：赤／品種：ピノタージュ／価格：¥1,250（税別）

3. カセドラル・セラー カベルネ・ソーヴィニヨン
深く濃い赤紫色、樽熟成に由来する複雑な風味と凝縮された果実味が特徴的。バランスの良さから若くても楽しめる。
色：赤／品種：カベルネ・ソーヴィニヨン／価格：¥2,100（税別）

4. ルーデバーグ
新鮮で力強いベリー系の豊かな香りが広がり、やがて樽熟成によるスパイシーさが続く。口あたりは滑らかで、力強さが堪能できる。
色：赤／品種：カベルネ・ソーヴィニヨンなど／価格：¥1,600（税別）

製造元 KWV　輸入販売元 国分株式会社

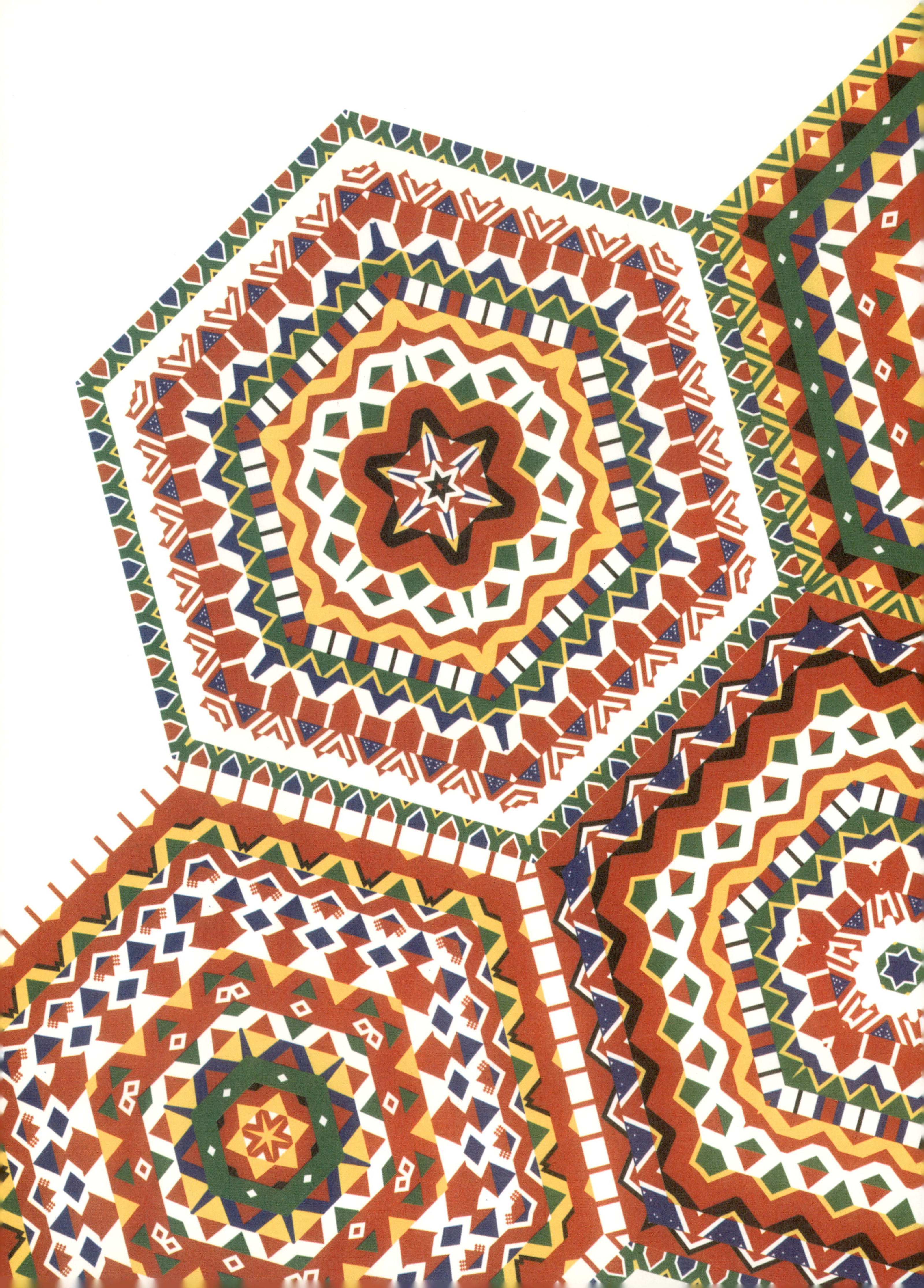

Perhaps you know about the greatest world design event? After creator Ravi Naidoo established Interactive Africa in 1994, Design Indaba started from the idea that creative power has become the motive power for South Africa's economic revolution. Thirteen years later, this image made Design Indaba develop into one of the world's highest-level design events. This event will include the invitation of creators from all over the world, relating to all fields of design. To understand Design Indaba, is something that is overwhelming, considering the large scale event that this organisation holds every year. Design Indaba is exactly Ravi Naidoo's knowledgeable inquisitiveness. Listen to one of the world's highest-level design inventor, Ravi Naidoo.

Interview with

Ravi Naidoo of DESIGN INDABA

Ravi Naidoo Profile

Nadioo completed his MBA at University of Cape Town before founding Interactive Africa in 1994, a Cape Town-based marketing and media company. Interactive Africa has assisted blue-chip clients in the sport, creative industries and high-tech sectors. Nadioo is also the co-founder of the Cape IT Initiative (CITI) and the International Design Indaba.

ケープタウン大学でMBAを取得。1994年にマーケティング・メディア会社Interactive Africaをケープタウンに設立。同社はスポーツ産業、クリエイティヴ産業、ハイテク産業における優良企業の支援を行なっている。またNadiooは、Cape IT Initiative（CITI）とDesign Indabaの共同創立者でもある。

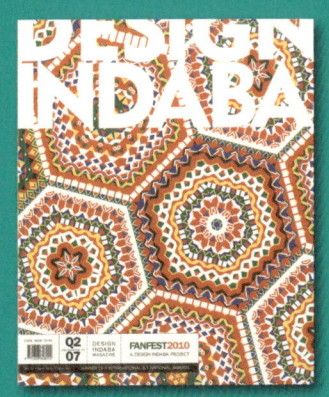

DESIGN INDABA MAGAZINE 2007

+81: What is Design Indaba?
Ravi Naidoo (RN): We at Design Indaba have committed the past 13 years to our vision, which strongly rests on the premise that creativity will fuel the economic revolution in South Africa. Design Indaba gathers the world's brightest talent across the creative industries - we have become a broad church for the graphic design, advertising, film, music, fashion design, industrial design, architecture, craft, visual art, new media, publishing, radio, television and performing arts sectors. This institution which incorporates events, media, education, training and business development, celebrated its tenth year in 2005. Design Indaba will expand into the South African Design Week next year, with the expo and conference program running over a week from 23 to 29 February, 2008.

+81: When and why did you start Design Indaba?
RN: We were inspired by the advent of democracy a decade ago, and wanted to play a role in helping to make South Africa work. At our company, Interactive Africa, we wanted to make a contribution beyond our day jobs - and knew that rather than just being concerned with our slice of the cake, we wanted to know how to make the cake bigger! We declared that the South African economy needed to lessen its dependency on commodities and begin to leverage its products and services globally. And we figured that design and innovation was a powerful lever for this. With this in mind, the plans for Design Indaba were developed with a few local designers and marketers. Over the years, Design Indaba has been faithful to its cause and its community, and this has given it immense credibility. It has been a relentless campaign for a decade, and we are still as passionate about it because we still have so much work to do. Design Indaba is a celebration of design in a country that has come to represent the triumph of the human spirit. Resurgent South Africa is a beacon to the world and is proof that even the most intractable problems can be neutralised by the will of people. The Design Indaba event typifies this optimism and a can-do spirit. It starts with the unselfish premise: How can design help solve the problems of an emerging country? It takes the view that we can create a better future by design.

+81: What do you think of the quality of South African design and art?
RN: It's gaining ground and getting its share of exposure, off a very small base. What we need to do now is create critical mass. Because if you look at the design media in SA, it seems that the same people are trotted out each time, 2-3 industrial designers, 6-8 graphic designers etc. And worryingly, given our apartheid past, they're almost all white! So we need to see this base increasing and becoming more representative of black South Africa. I am pinning my hopes on the youth - in this changing country, the energy now seems to come from the new guard, people who have gone to mixed schools and have benefited from a good education. That's what I see happening at our workshop series, which is why we place much store by it. Young designers jamming with creativity. When they hit the marketplace, you're going to hear about it.

+81: Can you tell us your future vision?
RN: Well, as we survey the global landscape, we see that more and more, the growth being generated by the successful economies is from the creative, value-added components. It represents about 30% of the US economy so its important that we hitch our economy to this motor.

Design Indaba 10 Conference

"Design Indaba 10 Conference, held annually in February, Cape Town at the Cape Town International Convention Centre. www.designindaba.com for more information or e-mail indaba@interactiveafrica.com"

世界最大級のデザイン・イベント「Design Indaba」を知っているだろうか？ 創設者のRavi Naidooは、1994年にInteractive Africaを設立した直後、クリエイティヴ力が南アフリカ経済革命の原動力になるという発想からDesign Indabaを立ち上げた。そして13年後、その想いはDesign Indabaを世界最大級のデザイン・イベントへと発展させた。デザインに関する全ての分野が網羅され、世界中からトップ・クリエイターが招かれるこのイベント。どこまでがDesign Indabaなのかを理解するのに戸惑うほどの大きな規模で毎年開催される。創設者であるNaidooの持つ知的好奇心がそのまま形になったものが、Design Indabaそのものなのだ。世界最大級のデザイン・イベンター Ravi Naidooに話を聞く。

+81：Design Indabaについて教えてください。
Ravi Naidoo（以下RN）：Design Indabaは、創造力こそが南アフリカ経済を向上させる源になるという考えのもと、13年間に渡り活動してきました。クリエイティヴ産業全体から世界で最も優れた人材が集まるDesign Indabaは、グラフィック・デザイン、広告、フィルム、出版、ラジオ、テレビ、舞台芸術といった分野のハブとしてその役割を担ってきました。またイベント、メディア、教育、トレーニング、ビジネスの向上の場としても機能し、2005年には創立10周年を迎えることができました。そして2008年2月23日〜29日に行なわれるSouth African Design Weekでは、展覧会やコンファレンスを一週間運営するなど、活動の場を広げています。

+81：Design Indabaをスタートした理由は？
RN：10年前の民主主義への移行に衝撃を受け、南アフリカが正常に機能するよう手助けをしたいと思ったのがきっかけです。私の会社であるInteractive Africaでは、仕事を超えて貢献できるようなことをしたかったのです。そしてほんのわずかな貢献に関わっているよりも、貢献できることをどうにかして増やしていきたいと思うようになっていったのです。

私たちはまず、南アフリカ経済は商品へ頼ることなく、世界的レベルでサービスや製品を展開する必要があると言明しました。デザインと新しいアイデアこそが現状を打破する強力な武器になると思ったのです。それを念頭に、地元の数人のデザイナーとマーケティング担当者と共に、Design Indabaの構想を成熟させていったのです。その原理と地域社会に対する忠実な態度を長年保持したことにより、大きな信頼を獲得しました。この10年間徹底した活動を続け、現在も情熱を持ってやるべき問題に取り組んでいます。

Design Indabaは一国のデザインを称えるものであり、結果として人間の精神の勝利をも意味しているのです。再起した南アフリカは世界の指針として、また困難な問題であっても人々の意思によって解決できるということを立証しています。このイベントは楽観主義となせばなる精神を象徴していると言えるでしょう。「どうやったらデザインが新興国の抱える問題を解決することができるか」というシンプルな発想からスタートし、デザインでよりよい将来を築いていこうと考えています。

+81：南アフリカのデザインとアートの特徴を教えてください。
RN：確実に前進し、日の目を見るようになってきました。私たちがこれから取り組まなければならないことはその人数を増やしていくこと。南アフリカのデザイン系メディアを例に挙げてみると、インダストリアル・デザイナーは2、3人、グラフィック・デザイナーは6〜8人といったように、同じ人が繰り返し登場するような状態です。アパルトヘイトの名残もあり、そういった人々のほとんどが白人。私たちは数字の底上げをして、南アフリカの黒人社会を象徴するようなものを作る必要があります。私はその希望を若者たちに見ています。白人と黒人が共に学ぶ学校へ通い、良い教育を受けた若者から、国を変えるようなエネルギーが生まれているように思えるのです。私たちが行なっているワークショップでもそういった傾向を見ることができ、だからこそワークショップの運営に力を入れているのです。若いクリエイターたちは創造力で溢れています。彼らがマーケットに姿を見せたとき、あなたもその名を耳にするでしょう。

+81：あなたが描く未来像を教えてください。
RN：私たちは世界の動向を観察していますが、好調な経済はクリエイティヴや付加価値商品から生じており、その傾向はどんどん顕著になってきています。アメリカの経済ではおよそ30%がそれらに相当しているほど。南アフリカ経済をこの原動力に繋げていくことはとても重要なのです。

The Design Indaba Expo

The Design Indaba Conference

The first International Design Indaba(R) conference was held in Cape Town in 1995. Subsequent Design Indabas have gone from strength to strength and they have played host to some of the world's super creatives, including David Carson, Neville Brody, Herman Zapf, Paula Scher, Karim Rashid, Ross Lovegrove, Terri Jones, Oliviero Toscani, Vince Frost, Sir Terence Conran, Stefan Sagmeister, Shigeru Ban, Naoto Fukasawa, Javier Mariscal, Brian Eno, Jasper Morrison and more. Over the past three years, the Design Indaba Conference has shown a dramatic increase in the number of delegates attending, with this year's event playing host to a capacity 2,664 delegates. Increasingly, the conference has also become a platform for local designers and creatives who are able to take their place on stage next to some of the thought-leaders of the world.

The Design Indaba Expo

In 2004, the Design Indaba Expo was inaugurated. The Expo component of the Design Indaba provides a commercial platform for the finest South African designers to leverage local goods and services to the global market. It also introduces the most influential international buyers to the finest South African creative product and encourages export. Its impact is also registered on the local market. The Expo aims to create discerning consumers through exposure to the principles and products of good design, resulting in the demand and production of innovative, evolving and excellent South African creative product. In 2007, the Design Indaba played host to 20,755 people over three days, including 260 Exhibitors and 137 International & Local buyers. For the exhibitors, the Expo was an encouraging success story both as a marketing platform and an opportunity to grow commercial and retail support, both locally and internationally.

第1回目の国際的規模のDesign Indabaは1995年にケープタウンで開催された。その後、回を重ねるごとに勢いを増し、世界のトップ・クリエイターたち（David Carson、Neville Brody、Herman Zapf、Paula Scher、Karim Rashid、Ross Lovegrove、Terri Jones、Oliviero Toscani、Vince Frost、Sir Terence Conran、Stefan Sagmeister、Shigeru Ban、深沢直人、Javier Mariscal、Brian Eno、Jasper Morrisonなど）を招くようになる。過去3年ではDesign Indaba Conferenceの参加者は急増し、2007年度は2,664名が参加。世界の学識者たちと共にカンファレンスに出席できるとあって、国内のデザイナーやクリエイターたちの意見発表の場としても成熟をみせている。

Design Indaba Expoは2004年に発足。Design Inbadaの博覧会は、南アフリカの最高のデザイナーの発表の場として、国内の商品やサービスをグローバル市場へ紹介する場として機能していいる。同時に、世界で最も影響力のあるバイヤーたちに、南アフリカの最良の製品を紹介し、輸出を促す場でもある。この影響は現地の市場にも大きな影響をもたらしている。博覧会は、よいデザインやその原理を発表することにより、先見のある消費者を作り出すことを目的にしており、結果的に需要、斬新な製品と発展、卓越した南アフリカ産の製品を促している。2007年度のDesign Inbadaには、3日間で出展者260名、国内外のバイヤー137名を含む20,755人が参加。出展者にとって博覧会は、国内外におけるマーケティングの場、また小売りのサポートや商売の拡大という両面において強力なバックアップとなっている。

Ravi Naidoo of **DESIGN INDABA**

Themba Mngomezulu started with the Darkie brand in 2000, and participated in the South Africa Fashion Week with his symbolic street fashion brand. The founder and creative director, Mngomezulu; men's designer, ladies designer, graphic designer, branding, and specialist at assigning roles for a functioning team. He has administered the mass production of the complete process, taking full responsibility of sewing patterns, and designs in a one floor style to realize an ideal house. He has brought to life youthful and desirable South African fashion from the chaotic, and a vast number of trial works, made of fabrics and patterns. We visited his factory and atelier located a slight distance from central downtown.

2000年、Themba MngomezuluによりスタートしたDarkieブランドは、South Africa Fashion Weekに参加するストリート・ファッション・ブランドのシンボル的存在である。創始者でクリエイティヴ・ディレクターであるMngomezuluとメンズデザイナー、レディースデザイナー、グラフィック・デザイナー、ブランディングと専門的に職域分担しながら、チームとして機能している。ワンフロアで、企画からデザイン、パターン、縫製、量産と全行程を管理しながら生産し、全てに責任を持つというメゾンの理想形態を実現している。おびただしい数の試作品に生地や型紙、この混沌から南アフリカの若者の求めるファッションが生まれる。ダウンタウンの中心部から少し離れたWood Stockにあるアトリエ兼ファクトリーを訪ねた。

Interview with

Themba Mngomezulu of Darkie

+81: How have you got into the fashion industry?
Themba Mngomezulu (TM): I shall say my mother brought me in. She used to sell second hand clothes and I sold them with her. Then naturally, I started to recycle my own shirts and pants. I gave myself over to sell and learned how to construct and govern the company.

+81: Can you tell us about the concept behind your fashion?
TM: I recycle a lot. Every entire collection based on the recycled stuff. Also make sure everybody understand our brand, what is our brand about, where we go, and what stands for. Each season we try to change what's been done before.

+81: Can you tell us about the concept of 07-08S/S collection?
TM: The concept is a barber shop including haircut, anything what you can do in salon.

+81: Where do you get inspiration?
TM: I draw my inspiration from what surrounds me like a guy waiting for a taxi, passengers in a public bus, homeless people, old furniture. I go to a small town and township to see people who live there and sometimes design according to their needs. It makes me aware of different life is now, I used to live in those areas before. Sometimes I miss it.

+81：どのようにしてファッション業界に入ったのですか？
Themba Mngomezulu（以下TM）：母の影響でこの業界に入ったと言っていいでしょう。彼女は古着屋を営んでいて、僕もよく店に出ていました。そうしているうちに自然とシャツやパンツをリメイクするようになったのです。洋服を売ることに夢中になり、ショップ運営のノウハウはそこから学びました。

+81：ブランドのコンセプトを教えてください。
TM：リサイクルです。すべてのコレクションはリサイクルに基づいています。また全ての人たちにブランドやその方向性、また何を表しているのかを理解してもらおうと思っています。毎シーズン、過去と違うことをしようと努力しています。

+81：07-08S/Sコレクションのコンセプトは何ですか？
TM：理髪店がテーマで、ヘアーカットなどヘアーサロンで出来ること全てに注目しました。

+81：インスピレーションの源を教えてください。
TM：身の回りにある全ての事柄からインスピレーションを得ます。例えば、タクシーを待つ人、公共バスの乗車客、ホームレス、古い家具からも。小さな町やタウンシップに行っては住民に会い、彼らの必要に応じて洋服をデザインすることもあります。僕は昔そうした町に住んでいたので、時に懐かしく感じ、今は違う人生を歩んでいることに気づかされます。

Themba Mngomezulu Profile

Born in 1977 in Pretoria, South Africa. While recycling a lot of clothes, Themba Mngomezulu started to customize and recycle clothes for his friends. Studied fashion design by himself. By just following the idea coming from his mind, he naturally started his carrier as a fashion designer. Darkie was founded in 2002. Moved to Cape Town in 2004.
www.darkieclothing.co.za

1977年、南アフリカのプレトリアに生まれる。何着もの洋服をリメイクするうちに、友人のためにカスタマイズを始め、独学でファッション・デザインの技術を習得。頭に浮かぶアイデアに従ってデザインしているうちに、自然とファッション・デザイナーの道を辿るようになる。2002年にDarkieをスタートし、2004年にケープ・タウンへ移住。

Themba Mngomezulu of **Darkie**

The brand Maya Prass for the South Africa Collection is attracting a great deal of attention. Each collection is gaining greater recognition with a fresh combination of an array of colors, print and fabric, that coordinate with accessories, which brim with African taste. The developing brand Maya Prass is representative of South African fashion, and is the work of a young 23 year old, who debuted at the Fashion Week in 2000. Maya Prass has produced a collection of creative colors, prints, and silhouettes with feminine charm. Despite the busy period before the release of the collection, she willingly gave us an interview. She is a cheerful, and charming young South African woman who holds much promise.

South Africa Collectionで、今最も注目を集めているブランドがMaya Prassである。カラフルな色使い、プリントとファブリックの新鮮な組み合わせ、そしてアフリカン・テイスト溢れるアクセサリーのコーディネートでコレクションごとにその評価はあがっている。2000年のFashion Weekに23歳の若さでデビューを果たし、今では南アフリカのファッション・シーンを代表するブランドに成長した。彼女が生み出すシルエット、プリント、カラーが、フェミニンな魅力のあるコレクションを作り上げている。コレクション前の忙しい時期にもかかわらず、快くインタビューを受けてくれた。笑顔のチャーミングな南アフリカ・ファッション期待の若手である。

Interview with

Maya Prass

+81: Please tell us the concept behind your creations.
Maya Prass (MA): I've worked on two collections. There are three really important elements: colour, print, and telling a story.

+81: Can you tell us concept for the 07-08 S/S collection?
MA: I'd say it's a sort of breaking down into many different feelings. The main concept is the ocean. I thought about travelling, discovering, and so on. I expressed them using fabric and shape.

+81: Do you think work is influenced by South Africa?
MA: Absolutely! I'd say South Africa is part of me. I love everything here. It gives me inspiration and influence.

+81: Can you tell us about the current South African fashion scene?
MA: It's a really interesting and exciting scene. It's also good place for people to start their career as a designer. Because it's such a small fashion industry and people are so hungry for new and exciting things. Unfortunately, though, local designers hardly get into international industries.

+81: What is your future vision?
MA: There are two things. One is scaling up my activities to abroad and the other is having my own store.

+81: クリエイションのコンセプトを教えてください。
Maya Prass (以下MA)：私は2つのラインを展開しているのですが、色、プリント、そしてストーリー性といった3つの要素を大切にしています。

+81：07-08 S/Sコレクションのコンセプトを教えてください。
MA：様々な感情を散りばめました。主なコンセプトは海。旅行や新たな発見などに着目し、それらを服の生地やシルエットで表現しています。

+81：あなたの作品は南アフリカの環境に影響されていると思いますか？
MA：もちろんです！南アフリカは私の一部であり、私はこの土地の全てを愛しています。また、インスピレーション源でもあるのです。

+81：最近の南アフリカのファッション・シーンについて聞かせてください？
MA：とても興味深く、エキサイティングだと思います。ここはデザイナーとしてのキャリアを始めるにはとても良い場所。なぜなら、まだ南アフリカのファッション業界は小さく、皆新しくてエキサイティングなことを求めているからです。しかしながら、地元のデザイナーが世界のファッション産業に入り込むのは厳しいと言えます。

+81：今後の計画を教えてください。
MA：1つは海外進出、もう1つは自分の店を持つことですね。

Maya Prass Profile

Launching her label in 2000, Maya Prass has become one of South Africa's top clothing designers. Her beautiful and wearable clothing is designed in collaboration with textile artists, and hand printed locally. Her work has been featured in top international publications and received South Africa's top fashion award, the Catherine Award.

2000年にレーベルを立ち上げ、現在は南アフリカを代表するトップ・デザイナーとなる。テキスタイル・アーティストとのコラボレーションによってデザインを行ない、現地でハンド・プリントする彼女の服作りは、着心地が良くて美しいと評判が高い。南アフリカで最高のファッション賞であるCatherine Awardを受賞、また海外の雑誌からも特集されている。

SOUTH AFRICA FASHION WEEK 2007-8 SS

Maya Prass

Andries Odendaal Profile

Cape Town-based new media designer and developer. Has worked on many commercial and experimental projects and is the programmer behind sites and projects like Wireframe.co.za. Also active in the web design community and the international conference circuit presenting. Co-author of the books "New Masters Of Flash" and "Flash 5 Studio".

ケープタウンを拠点に活動するメディア・デザイナーでありデベロッパー。コマーシャル・ワークや実験的なプロジェクトを数多く手がける。Wireframe.co.zaをはじめとするサイトや企画のプログラマーでもある。ウェブデザイン・コミュニティや世界的なカンファレンスにて活躍中。『New Masters Of Flash』と『Flash 5 Studio』を共著。

Most people probably know Andries Odendaal better as "Wire Fram". Based out of Cape Town, he is a developer of interactive media who is active worldwide as a lecturer and judge (D&AD and One Show). Almost everyone has seen at least one of his works somewhere as his unique concepts and fascinating compositions tend to draw people's attention. Known as one of the best Flash programmers in the world, his list of clients includes the Discovery Channel, National Geographic, Getty Images, Diesel, Hewlett Packard, the BBC, and the Science Museum London. We spoke with Odendaal about his works at a historic downtown café.

Andries Odendaalというよりも"Wire Fram"の名前でわかる人もいるだろう。彼はケープタウンをベースにしながら、世界中で講演や審査員（D&ADやOne Showなど）として活躍しているデザイナーであり、インタラクティヴ・メディアの開発者である。彼の作品はどこかで見たことのあるものが多い。そのユニークな発想と魅力的な構成には、思わず引き込まれるものばかりである。彼は世界最高のFlash Programmerのひとりとしても知られており、クライアントにはDiscovery Channel、National Geographic、Getty Images、Diesel、Hewlett Packard、BBC、Science Museum Londonなどが並ぶ。ダウンタウンにある歴史的なカフェで作品を見ながら話を聞いた。

Interview with

Andries Odendaal

+81: When did you start working as an interactive media designer?
Andries Odendaal (AO): Like many people in this industry, I was the proud owner of a C64 at the age of 12 and learned the basics of programming during this time. It was only much later in the mid 90's that I started pursuing this as a career.

+81: Please tell us about the concept of your works and your creative process.
AO: For me, mathematics, programming and user participation are as much part of the design process as what drawing a pixel is. At the moment my design draws a lot from both, sometimes starting with a visual idea, sometimes starting off as a line of code. I like the user to interact with my programs, and I try to produce work that is very playful in this respect.

+81: What does interactive design mean to you?
AO: I often try and create works that are open ended. I like the user to engage with his/her own creativity when confronted with my works. To me this is more interactive, because the user can actively participate and sometimes even contributes to the work itself.

+81: How do you feel about the environment of South Africa?
AO: South Africa has been a very positive place in the last 10 years. There's been lots of growth and one can notice the change all around the country. I'm excited to see where it will go.

+81：インタラクティブ・デザイナーになった経緯を教えてください。
Andries Odendaal（以下AO）：この業界にいる多くの人たちと同じように、12歳の時にC64を購入し、プログラミングの基礎を学びました。それからだいぶ経った90年代の半ばに、本格的にキャリアをスタートしました。

+81：仕事におけるコンセプトと、その過程を教えてください。
AO：数学、プログラミング、ユーザー参加は、デザインをする過程においてピクセルを書くのに匹敵するぐらい大切です。現在は2通りのデザインの方法をとっていて、ビジュアル・アイデアから書き始める場合と、プログラムを書くことからはじめる場合があります。ユーザーがプログラムと交信し、その相互関係から遊び心のある作品を生み出すことを心がけています。

+81：あなたにとって、インタラクティブ・デザインとは何ですか？
AO：柔軟性のある作品を作るよう努力しています。ユーザーが作品を見たときに、自らの創造性で作品に共鳴してもらえると嬉しいです。このようにユーザーが積極的に参加できること、また時として作品に貢献してくれることが、私にとってのインタラクティブなのです。

+81：南アフリカの環境についてはどう感じていますか？
AO：南アフリカはこの10年間で大きく前進しました。全国で見られるその変化は、誰の目にも明らかです。これからどこに向かっていくのかとても楽しみです。

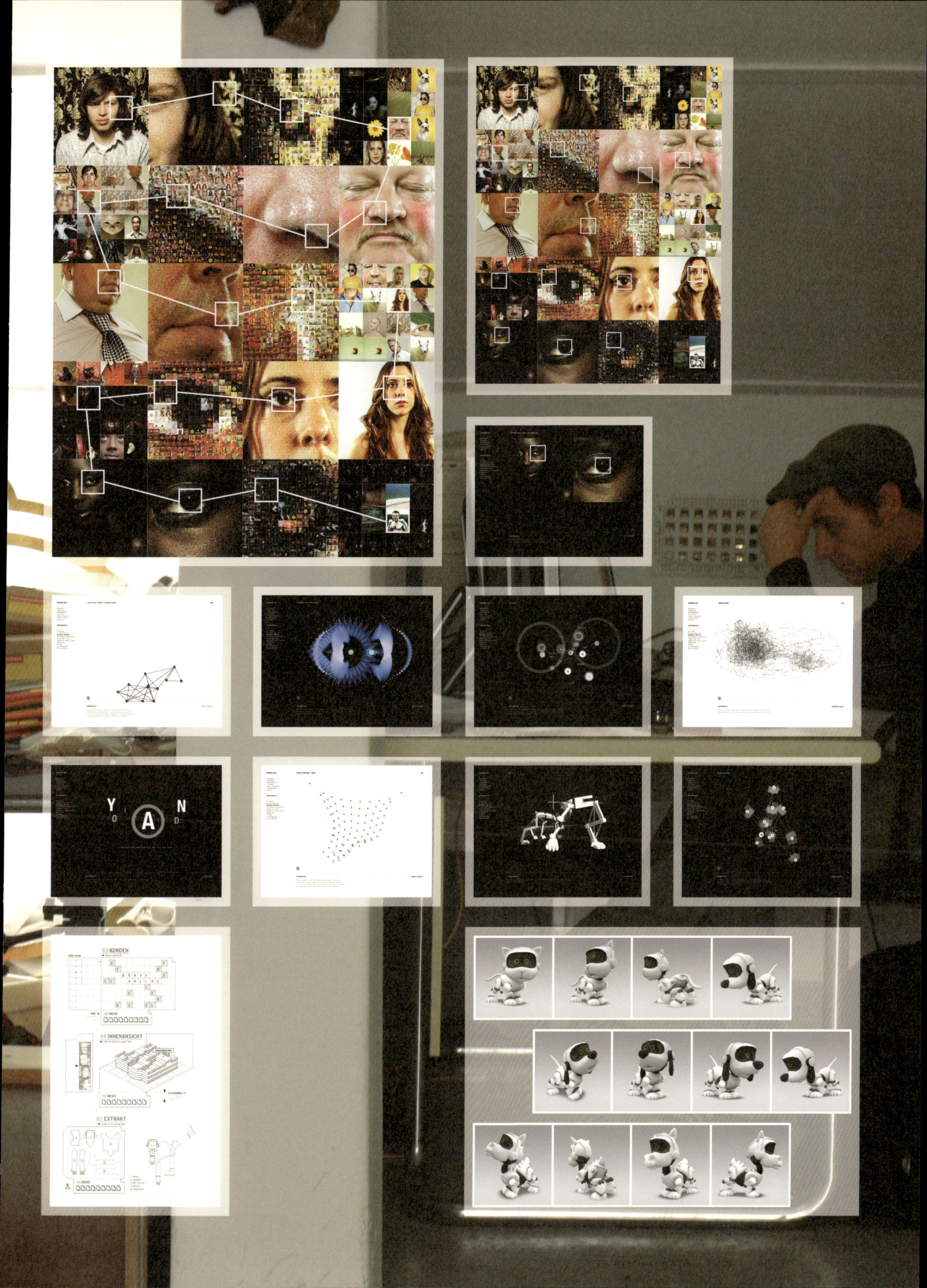
03 KUNDEN
04 INNENANSICHT
02 EXTRAKT

Comme des Garcons T-shirts Graphic design, and the cover of Idn magazine is a globally active Cape Town design studio. Rich in humor, the design that he created has been re-worked, having a charm and an instinctively comic softness. This is a designer who continues to create designs full of human awareness at extreme ends of the spectrum for classic design that have been digitalized. His studio, and 'Daddy Buy Me a Pony' exhibits are unique in design.

コムデギャルソンのT-shirtsグラフィック・デザインや「Idn magazine」の表紙など世界的に活躍するケープタウンのグラフィック・デザイン・スタジオ。ユーモアに富み、ひとひねり工夫された彼らが創りだすデザインは、思わず微笑んでしまう優しい魅力的なものである。デジタル化したグラフィック・デザインの対極に存在する人間味あふれるデザインを創り続けている。スタジオも作品もユニークなDaddy Buy Me a Ponyデザインを訪れた。

Interview with Peet Pienaar of Daddy Buy Me a Pony

Peet Pienaar & Heidi Chisholm Profile

Peet Pienaar started working as a graphic designer in 2001 and Heidi Chisholm started in 1995.

グラフィック・デザイナーとしてのキャリアは、Peet Pienaarが2001年に、Heidi Chisholmが1995年にスタートさせた。

+81: Tell us the concept of your works and your creative process.
Peet Pienaar (PP): Non conscious African design is the basis of our design, we are not interested in western design or western design principals. We always try to use alternative printing processes like flocking and glitter silk screening to create work that people want to keep.

+81: What does graphic design mean to you?
PP: Graphic design is a tool to change the world around us, to change people's perception about Africa.

+81: What do you feel about the environment of South Africa?
PP: South Africa with its huge history and many cultures is one of the most inspiring places in the world, we wouldn't want to be anywhere else right now.

+81：作品のコンセプトや制作過程を教えてください。
Peet Pienaar（以下PP）：無意識の中でのアフリカ・デザインが、私たちのデザインの基本。西洋のデザインやデザイン原理には興味がありません。人々がずっと持っていたくなるような作品作りを目指して、フロック加工やグリッター・シルクスクリーンなどを用いた新しい印刷工程に挑戦しています。

+81：あなたにとってグラフィック・デザインとは何ですか？
PP：グラフィック・デザインは自分たちの世界を変えることができる、そして人々が抱くアフリカの認識を変えるためのツールです。

+81：南アフリカの環境についてどうのように感じていますか？
PP：長い歴史と様々な文化が混じり合う南アフリカは、世界の中でも最も活気のある場所のひとつ。今は他の場所へ移動する気はありませんね。

Peet Pienaar of **Daddy Buy Me a Pony**

HOTSPOTS
FOR SAHA
RUNDETÅ
17. AUGUST
30. SEPTEM

Stefan Antoni

Stefan Antoni Profile

On graduating from the University of Cape Town in 1985, he worked for a local firm. Due to the recession there was little work so Antoni decided to set up his own practice. Today it employs over 80 staff and has projects not only in South Africa but Senegal, the Seychelles, Abu Dhabi, Switzerland and France.

1985年にケープタウン大学卒業後、1年間地元の会社で勤務。不景気で仕事が少なかったため、自ら会社を設立する。現在は80人ものスタッフを抱え、南アフリカのみならず、セネガル、セーシェル、アブダビ（アラブ首長国連邦）、スイス、フランスにまで事業を拡大している。

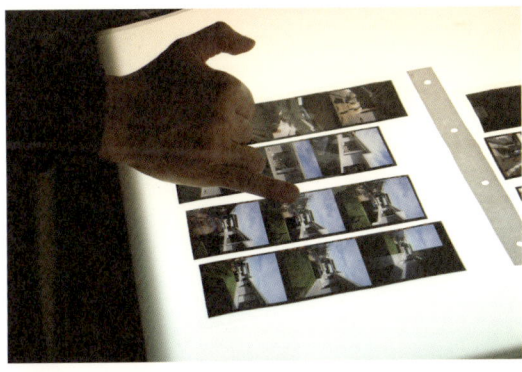

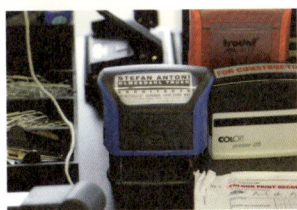

Stefan Antoni is Cape Town's leading architect, constructing beautiful and elegant housing. A residence gives the feeling that it's for an elegant lifestyle with a sea view and a sea breeze. It is plain to see why you would want to have your house built by Stefan Antoni. His area of work is not only confined to residential housing, however, he continues to expand his area of work, from hotels to leisure facilities, to architectural design overseas. We visited his newly relocated studio.

華麗で優雅な住宅を設計する、ケープタウンを代表する建築家。海と潮風を感じさせる優雅なライフスタイルが、目の前に現れてくるかのような住宅である。なぜ彼に住まいの設計を依頼したくなるかは一目瞭然である。彼らの仕事の領域は住宅のみならず、ホテル、レジャー施設から国外の建築設計まで広がり続けている。移転したばかりの新しいスタジオを訪ねた。

Interview with

Stefan Antoni

+81: Please tell us the concept of your works and your process of making.
Stefan Antoni (SA): One of our strengths is that we put a lot of effort into understanding our clients and their particular lifestyles. It is a lot easier now, as most clients are already attracted to projects we have done and enjoy the flowing open contemporary feel. We like to keep the design simple but not too boring or plain. We love a layered feel and the making of great spaces. We prefer not to just design boxes but spaces that interrelate creating exciting and dynamic experiences. Light is very important - whether through large openings, under deep overhangs or through slots in the roof. With our wonderful climate, a seamless interface between indoor and outdoor living is essential.
My two business partners Greg Truen, Philip Olmesdahl and I design most projects - either together - or with a small group dedicated to each project. Analyzing the site, the brief and budget are key components to starting the process successfully. We all have similar interests and taste so we normally improve on each others ideas. We like our projects to have a quiet but strong character and try to avoid any forms or details that are not timeless.

+81: What do you think of the quality of South African architecture?
SA: People are often quite surprised and impressed by the quality of South African Architecture. Commercial and public architecture tends to go to the same commercial firms so this is often not as exciting as domestic architecture, where clients are very demanding and expect to meet international standards. Construction skills are currently in limited supply, as we are experiencing a major construction boom. The standard of University education is high but unfortunately many students leave to work overseas after graduating. A number of them return but not enough.

+81: What do you feel about the environment of South Africa?
SA: South Africa is undoubtedly one of the most beautiful countries in the world with majestic mountains, beautiful coastlines, jungles, deserts, wild animals - we have virtually everything here. A major necessity at the moment is the provision of houses, schools, clinics and other services as well as education. A vibrant middle class is essential to the success of the country.

+81: What's your future vision?
SA: South Africa has an enormous potential. We need to look after all the skills we have in the country and develop more skills as quickly as possible. Tourism is very strong and being a beautiful and stable country I have no doubt that in the long term it will develop into a superb and dynamic environment to live and work in. We are very excited about our role in developing South Africa to it's full potential and setting an example through our work to the rest of the world.

+81：仕事におけるコンセプトと建築物を作る過程を教えてください。
Stefan Antoni（以下SA）：私たちの強みは、クライアントのライフスタイルを深く理解することに力を注いでいるという点です。現在は、ほとんどのクライアントが、我々が今までに手がけてきたプロジェクトに興味を持ち、またコンテンポラリーなものに対して理解されてきたので、昔よりずっと楽になりました。建築デザインは常にシンプルなものにしたいと思っていますが、何の変哲もないつまらないものにはしたくありません。また、幾層も造ってそこに空間を創り出すのが好きです。ただ「箱」をデザインするのではなく、興奮やダイナミズムを体験できるような「空間」のデザインを心がけたいですね。それから、光はとても重要です。たとえそれが大きな窓から入ってくる光でも、深い張り出しからさす光や、屋根の細い隙間からさす光であっても、非常に重要な役割を果たします。素晴らしい気候を持つ南アフリカでは、野外と屋内の境界がないような住居が必要不可欠です。
仕事に関しては、ビジネス・パートナーであるGreg TruenとPhilip Olmesdahl、私の3人が一緒になって、もしくは小さなグループを組んでプロジェクトを遂行していきます。敷地の分析、概要、予算といった重要な要素を分析することが、仕事をスムーズに進め、成功に導きます。我々全員が似たようなものに興味を持ち、センスも近いので、お互いに切磋琢磨しながらアイデアを向上させていくようにしています。私たちのプロジェクトは、派手過ぎないけれども強い個性を持っているので、一時的な形式や細かい事にとらわれることなくやっていきたいですね。

+81：南アフリカの建築の特性についてどうお考えですか？
SA：外国の人は、よく良質な南アフリカの建築に驚いたり、感嘆します。クライアントは国際的な基準を期待して厳しく注文を付けるのですが、実際商業用の建築物や、公的な建築物の大半が、似たり寄ったりです。建設の技術に関しても、今日の建築ブームのため、供給が限られています。大学での教育レベルはとても高いのですが、残念ながら多くの生徒は卒業後に海外へ働きに出て行ってしまいますね。何人もの生徒が戻ってきますが、その数は十分とは言えません。

+81：南アフリカの環境についてどう思いますか？
SA：南アフリカは間違いなく、世界で最も美しい国の一つだと思います。雄大な山、美しい海岸線、ジャングル、砂漠、野生の動物など、全てがここに存在します。また、教育と同じように、家、学校、病院、その他のサービスの供給が現在最も必要です。活気のある中流階級が、この国を発展に導くカギを握っているでしょう。

+81：将来の方向性を教えてください。
SA：南アフリカは膨大な可能性を秘めていると思います。私たちの持っている全ての技術に磨きをかけ、できるだけ早いスピードで技術をさらに発展させていかなければならないと思います。観光業は非常に強く、美しく安定した国なので、長期的に見ると住むのにも働くのにもとても活気に満ちた、素晴らしい環境になると信じています。南アフリカの発展に貢献しているという我々の役割に非常に情熱を持っていますし、最大限の力を出して、今後他国の手本になるようにしていきたいですね。

Stefan Antoni

Waltons
W36C
mma
project
client
file 01
mma
project
client
file 01
mma
project
client
file 01
mma
project
client
File 01
mma
project
client
file 01

Interview with

Luyanda Mpahlwa

Luyanda Mpahlwa has handled state architectural projects, the design of the South African consulate in Berlin, and the design of the Cape Town football stadium for the World Cup in 2010. He proceeds with large-scale projects, while others are not yet finished. Whilst life has its difficulties, he continuously thrusts forward with his passion towards architecture and his love of the Republic of South Africa. We visited his office in Cape Town.

ベルリンの南アフリカ大使館の設計から、2010年ワールドカップのケープタウン・フットボール・スタジアムの設計、国家プロジェクト建築の設計まで手がけるLuyanda Mpahlwa。プロジェクトが終わらないうちに大規模な新プロジェクトが進められている。紆余曲折な人生を送りながらも、南アフリカ共和国への愛と建築に対する情熱が彼を前へ前へと突き進めて行くのだろう。ケープタウンの彼のオフィスを訪ねた。

Luyanda Mpahlwa Profile

Luyanda Mpahlwa went into exile in Germany in 1986 after serving time as a political prisoner on Robben Island. He completed his Master in Architecture in Berlin in 1997 and was coordinating architect with MMA Architects for the South African Embassy project there. He is now Principal and director of MMA Architects in Cape Town.

政治犯としてロベン島に服役した後、1986年ドイツへ亡命。97年、ベルリンにて建築の修士課程を修了。その後、ベルリンで行なわれた南アフリカ大使館のプロジェクトにおいて建築家としてMMA Architectsのコーディネーターを担当。現在はケープタウンのMMA Architectsにてディレクター兼社長を務めている。

Green point Stadium 2010, Cape Town

The primary school in South Africa

Luyanda Mpahlwa

After being an overseas student in Los Angeles, Don Albert says he started soundspacedesign with the opportunity of designing the Millennium Tower in Durban, in 2000. After that, he was at the center of handling commercial facility design, and he has set up offices in Durban and Cape Town. We look forward to future activities from this young group of architects

ロス留学からの帰国後、2000年にコンペによりダーバンのMillennium Towerの設計を契機にsoundspacedesignをスタートしたとDon Albertは語る。その後、彼らは商業施設設計を中心に手がけ、ケープタウンとダーバンに事務所を構えるまでになった。若き建築家集団のこれからの活躍を楽しみにしたい。

Interview with Don Albert of soundspacedesign

Don Albert Profile

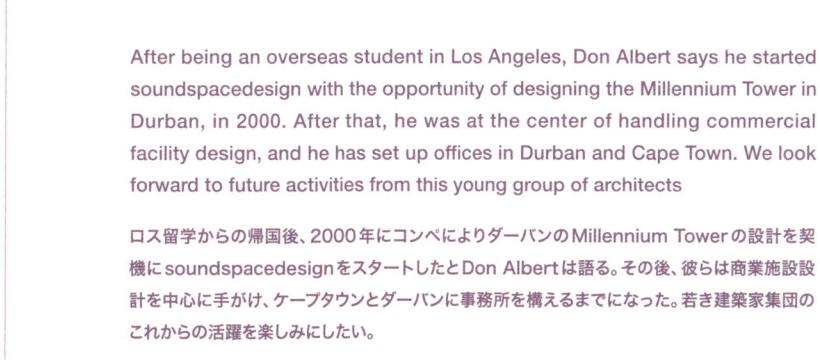

Graduating from the University of Natal, Don Albert then completed an MA in architecture at the University of California, during which time he set up soundspacedesign. On returning to South Africa in 1999, Albert has had internationally published projects, he lectures widely and has introduced to column inches in respected architecture publications.

Natal大学卒業後、カリフォルニア大学の建築科の修士課程を修了。その間に建築事務所soundspacedesignを設立する。1999年に南アフリカに帰国し、国際的なプロジェクトを遂行してきた中で、幅広い分野で講義をし、また名誉ある建築関連の出版物にも多々取り上げられている。

soundspacedesign Profile

Established in 1998, soundspacedesign submitted the winning design for the Millennium Tower, Durban, the highperformancecentre at the University of Pretoria, and the Proud Heritage Clothing Campus, Durban. In 2003, it relocated to Cape Town, and currently employs four architects. Recent proposals include a soccer theme park and a private air terminal in Gauteng.

1998年に設立されたsoundspacedesignは、Millennium Tower（ダーバン）、プレトリア大学のhighperformancecentre、そしてProud Heritage Clothing Campus（ダーバン）で賞を受賞してきた。2003年には拠点をケープ・タウンに移し、現在は4人の建築家を抱えている。近年では、サッカーのテーマパーク、及びハウテン州にある私営の空港ターミナルの建設を予定している。

+81: Please tell us the concept of your works and your process of making.
Don Albert(DA): As an architect I am particularly inspired by nature and harmony, and an understanding of beauty from a mathematical perspective - much on the lines of Pythogoras, and many of the champions of Western Aesthetics, Leon Battista Alberti, Marcus Vitruvius Pollio and so on. Of course I believe that Eastern aesthetics have a similar "classical" understanding of proportion and harmony too and I am particularly inspired by Japanese concepts of spatial flow and separation. This same aesthetic understanding of harmony exists in music too, hence our interest in sound. What time is to music, is what space is to architecture. Every project at soundspacedesign is an opportunity to rethink architecture and urbanism. In some instances we do our research so well that the client ends up realizing that they didn't need to build a building at all!

+81: What do you think of the quality of South African architecture?
DA: There is a bit of a Wild West attitude in South Africa at the moment, due to the biggest sustained building boom in living memory, which has generally produced a lot of sub-standard environments from a design perspective. We at soundspacedesign are more interested in a critical approach that looks at universality and specificity with equal emphasis. Buildings must fit into their context but also have enough to offer the architectural discourse from a global perspective.

+81: What's your future vision?
DA: Architecture in South Africa should concern itself less with style and more with planning issues and the fabric of the city. The legacy of Apartheid Planning and its fragmented approach to land-use where people travel extraordinary distances to work is still with us and a major obstacle to access and upliftment. The potential of land-use and city form to influence positive growth, environmentally conscientious development and improved social relations needs to be reconsidered and architects should still be educating their clients in this regard. There are many towns in South Africa which have outlived their economic rationale for existence and are a strain on national infrastructure and social services. I see a more responsible urbanization taking hold where the larger urban centres are regenerated and town planning in the proper sense of the word comes back to forefront of city management.

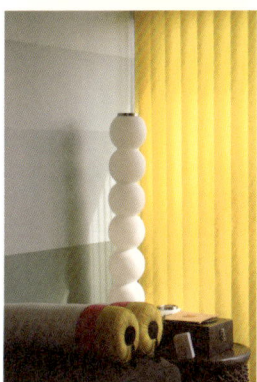

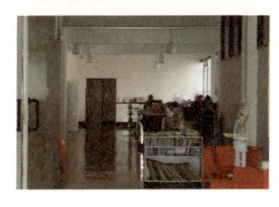

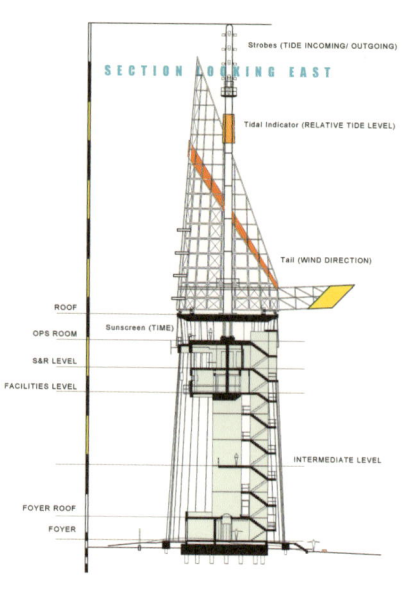

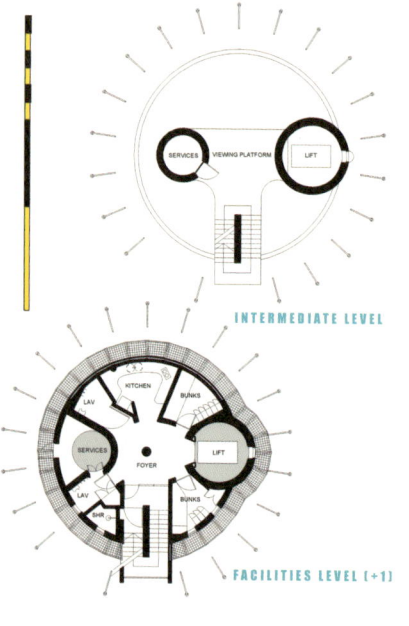

DURBAN'S MILLENNIUM TOWER National Ports Authority, Port of Durban

+81：仕事におけるコンセプトと建築物を作る過程を教えてください。
Don Albert（以下DA）：一建築家として、自然との調和を心がけています。また、ピタゴラスの定理に沿った線や、Leon Battista Alberti, Marcus Vitruvius Pollioなどの西洋の美意識を極めた建築家が持つ、数学的な美学に影響を受けています。もちろん東洋の美学も同じように、バランスや自然との調和を考えた古典的な思想を持っていると思いますし、空間の流れや分離を大切にする日本の建築からは私自身も間違いなく、影響を受けています。このような、調和を考えた美学というのは、音楽においても存在すると思うので、音に対しても同じく興味を持っています。音楽にとっての「時間」は、建築にとっての「空間」と同じです。またsoundspacedesignが手がける全てのプロジェクトが、建築と都会化について再考する機会になっています。例えば、我々は仕事をうける際に徹底的にリサーチをしますが、その結果クライアントが、そのビルを建てる必要が全くないという結論を出したことすらあります。

+81：南アフリカの建築の特性についてはどうお考えですか？
DA：現在の南アフリカでは、アメリカ開拓期のような風潮があり、かつてないほどの大きな建設ブームが巻き起こっています。それらの建築物はデザインの視点から言うと、多くのものが環境基準を下回っているのが現状です。我々soundspacedesignは、そういったことよりも普遍性と特殊性に対し同種の重要性を与えるという、ある種批判的なアプローチに関心を向けています。建築はその背景に適したものでなければならないと同時に、グローバルな視点で語られなければなりません。

+81：将来の方向性を教えてください。
DA：南アフリカの建築は、スタイルよりももっと都市構造や計画を考慮していかなければならないと思います。アパルトヘイトの後遺症とその断片的な土地の利用法は、人々が今もなお、長距離を移動して働きに行かなければならなかったり、アクセスやバス通勤の大きな障害となっています。これからの土地利用と、発展につながる都市計画、そして環境を充分に考慮した発展と、社会的関係の改良について我々は再考していく必要があり、また建築家はそれをクライアントに教育していくべきだと考えています。南アフリカには、まだ経済的に不安定で、国のインフラやソーシャル・サービスが不十分な都市がたくさんあります。私はより大きな都市部の施設を再建することで、都市化を確固たるものにし、本当の意味での都市計画を最前線で進めていかなければならないという使命を感じています。

BARROWS - Point of Sale Factory - Durban 19 Intersite Avenue, Umgeni Business Park

CLOTHING DESIGN AND DISTRIBUTION CENTRE PROUD HERITAGE CAMPUS Durban

Don Albert of **soundspacedesign**

Heidi Erdmann Profile

Heidi Erdmann has worked as curator and dealer of photography for the past ten years. She owns the Photographers Gallery za in Cape Town, South Africa where she represents amongst others, George Hallett, Paul Alberts, Roger Ballen, Lien Botha, Pieter Badenhorst, Jean Brundrit, Jurgen Schadeberg and Grada Djeri.

写真関係のキュレーターやディーラーを10年間務めた後、ケープタウンにThe Photographers Gallery zaをオープン。George Hallett、Paul Alberts、Roger Ballen、Lien Botha、Pieter Badenhorst、Jean Brundrit、Jurgen Schadeberg、Grada Djeriなど、南アフリカのアーティストを軸としたキュレーションを手がける。

South African photography (a brief overview)

Photography today is central in contemporary art. It has become the most sought after medium and this decade alone has seen more photographs being produced for gallery walls and museum exhibitions than any other time. Nowadays no exhibition is complete without the inclusion of photography. However, the development of photography as an accepted art form in South Africa has been much slower. The country has a long history of social documentary photography, and many of the practitioners of the 1950's and 1960's have become world acclaimed, amongst them Jurgen Schadeberg, Peter Makubane and David Goldblatt.

During the 1970 and 1980 social documentary had become the most dominant genre in South African photography. It had also become the most powerful tool to affect political change. During the 1980's there was a nationwide State of Emergency and ordinary South Africans needed their stories of suffering to be seen.

By the 1990's the political climate had changed and so did the visual language of South African photography. Without the collective political purpose many photographers were left with a creative void. It was time for new stories to be told and for a new visual language to unfold. I consider this era as the most fascinating period of South African contemporary photography.

Issues such as identity, environmental concerns, AIDS, issues surrounding gender and sexuality had now become the focal points in works by a whole new breed of photographers. This era also saw the introduction of conceptual photography.

The Photographers Gallery za was established in 2001 as a platform to showcase contemporary South African photography. Through regular exhibitions, and working with a wide variety of photographers, the idea was to create an environment for the development of new trends and visual languages in the local market.

今日、写真は現代アートの中心に据えられている。最も人気のあるツールとなり、今世紀はかつてないほどたくさんの写真がギャラリーの壁を覆い、美術館での展覧会のために制作されている。写真なしでは展覧会が成り立たないと言っても過言ではない。しかしながら、南アフリカにおいて写真がアートとして認知されるまで、比較的時間がかかっている。この国には社会派ドキュメンタリー写真の長い歴史があり、Jurgen Schadeberg、Peter Makubane、David Goldblattをはじめとする50年代、60年代の先人たちが世界中から注目を浴びていた。

70年代、80年代と南アフリカの写真シーンにおいて、社会派ドキュメンタリーが主力となった。また、それが政治的な変化をもたらす最強手段でもあった。80年代には非常事態宣言が発令され、南アフリカ市民は辛酸を舐めてきた日々が日の目を見ることを望んでいたのだ。

90年代までには政治情勢が一変し、南アフリカの写真は視覚言語として用いられるようになった。集団的な政治目的は別として、たくさんのフォトグラファーがクリエイティヴへの虚無感を抱くようになっていった。それは新しい歴史について語られ、視覚言語が発達する時期でもあり、思えば南アフリカの現代写真史において最も輝いた時代であった。

アイデンティティ、環境問題、エイズ、そしてジェンダーと性差。このような問題は、新進系のフォトグラファーたちにとって、現在極めて重要なポイントになっている。そして、コンセプチュアルな写真が導入された時期でもある。

The Photographers Gallery zaは南アフリカ現代写真の発表空間の基軸として、2001年に設立された。定期的に展覧会を行ない、様々なフォトグラファーたちと活動展開している。コンセプトは、土地に根ざしたアート市場に新しいトレンド、ならびに視覚言語が発達するための基盤を作ることである。

1. George Hallett
First encounter, Johannesburg
Silver gelatine hand print
Edition /25
40 x 50 cm
1994

2. Pierre Crocquet
Fate
forms part of the Love First series
Silver gelatin hand-prints
Edition /7
57 x 45.5 cm
2006

3. Dale Yudelman
Beach
forms part of Reality Bytes series
Colour Lambda photograph
Edition /15
36 x 55 cm
2006

4. Geoffrey Grundlingh
Untitled
forms part of the Utopia series
Colour Lambda photographs
Edition /5
42.5 x 51 cm
2001

Strijdom van der Marwe continues to produce conceptual art on natural canvass. These exhibits have been realized with a concept of putting emphasis on a process of production. One can understand the idea behind this magnificent project and Strijdom's production aim, when one views his exhibits, which have an extremely beautiful appearance. Similar exhibits speak in mild tones. This is an artist that lets you feel his passion towards his core creative inner strength.

自然をキャンパスにコンセプチュアルなアート作品を作り続けるStrijdom van der Marwe。作品そのものよりも、コンセプトを実現させるための制作過程に重きを置く。見た目の美しさ以上に、作品を並べて見るときに、彼の制作意図と壮大なプロジェクトの発想を理解することができる。作品同様、温和な口調で語りながら、その芯の強さとクリエイティヴに対する情熱を感じさせてくれるアーティストである。

Interview with

Strijdom van der Marwe

Strijdom van der Marwe Profile

Recipient of the Jackson Pollock-Krasner Foundation Grant, Medal of Honor from the South African Academy of Arts and Science, he has had exhibitions and commissions in South Korea, Belgium, France, Sweden, and Japan. In recent years and his work has been bought by numerous private and public collectors, locally and abroad.

Jackson Pollock-Krasner財団から助成金を受け、South African Academy of Arts and Scienceからは名誉勲章を授与される。これまで韓国、ベルギー、フランス、スウェーデン、日本などで展覧会を開催し、制作依頼を受ける。近年では国内外、プロ・アマを問わず多くのコレクターから支持を受けている。

+81: Can you tell us the concept behind your photographs?
Strijdom van der Marwe (SVM): Firstly, the picture must be wonderful and beautiful to look at. In order to have the same vision as viewer, the artist must understand very well why the picture was shoot in the specific place and moment. I often go out, I sit there for a while for a kind of meditation. The important thing is not the artwork itself, but also the process of the artwork.

+81: How do you feel about the South African art scene?
SVM: It has changed very much. When I was an art student, the government had no money to run the National Gallery. Suddenly, new galleries opened and artists exhibited freely. It was something new and exiting. On the other hand, people used to be hedged in their minds because of our history. Now we are free, but everyone has different way of thinking. For this reason, it's interesting being in this country.

+81: What is the special quality of the South Africa?
SVM: Geographically, Cape Town is an enriched city with fresh green, where two different oceans encounter each other. It's fantastic to work on all the different landscapes in one country.

+81: Please tell us about your future vision.
SVM: The biggest influence is not artist, but the landscape itself. I'm very interested in the global warming issue. So I'd love to try eco art.

+81：写真に潜むコンセプトについて教えてください。
Strijdom van der Marwe（以下SVM）：まず始めに写真というものは、見てわくわくする、美しいものでなければなりません。見る側とヴィジョンを共有するためには、作り手であるアーティストはどうしてその写真がある特定の場所、瞬間に撮られたかということをよく理解する必要があるのです。僕はよく外に出かけて、瞑想するようにしばらく座り込みます。作品だけではなく、その制作過程も重要なのです。

+81：南アフリカのアート・シーンはどのようにお考えですか？
SVM：すっかり変りましたね。私が美大生だった頃、国立美術館を運営するための政府の費用は底をついていました。すると突然、新しいギャラリーがオープンし、アーティストが自由に作品を展示出来るようになったのです。それはもう新鮮で心躍る出来事でした。またかつては、辛い歴史によって皆心を閉ざしていましたが、今は自由でそれぞれに違った考え方を持っています。だからこそ、この国は面白いのです。

+81：南アフリカの醍醐味とは？
SVM：ケープタウンは地理的にみると清々しい緑がある恵まれた街で、ふたつの異なる大海が交わる場所でもあります。ひとつの国で様々な風景を題材にできることは素晴らしいですね。

+81：将来的なヴィジョンについて教えてください。
SVM：一番の影響力はアーティストではなく、風景そのものです。地球温暖化問題にとても関心があるので、エコロジカル・アートに取り組んでいきたいです。

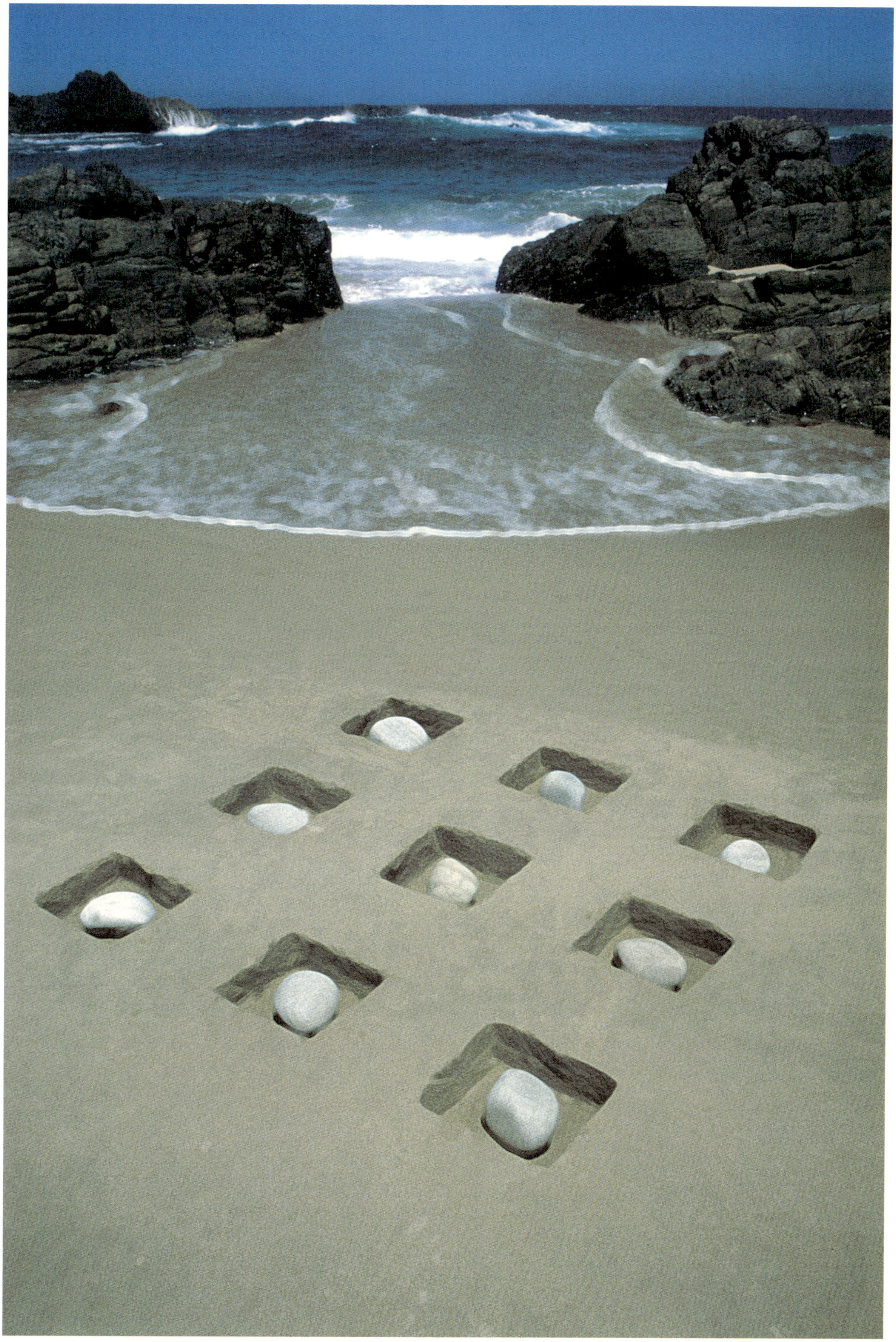

Strijdom van der Marwe

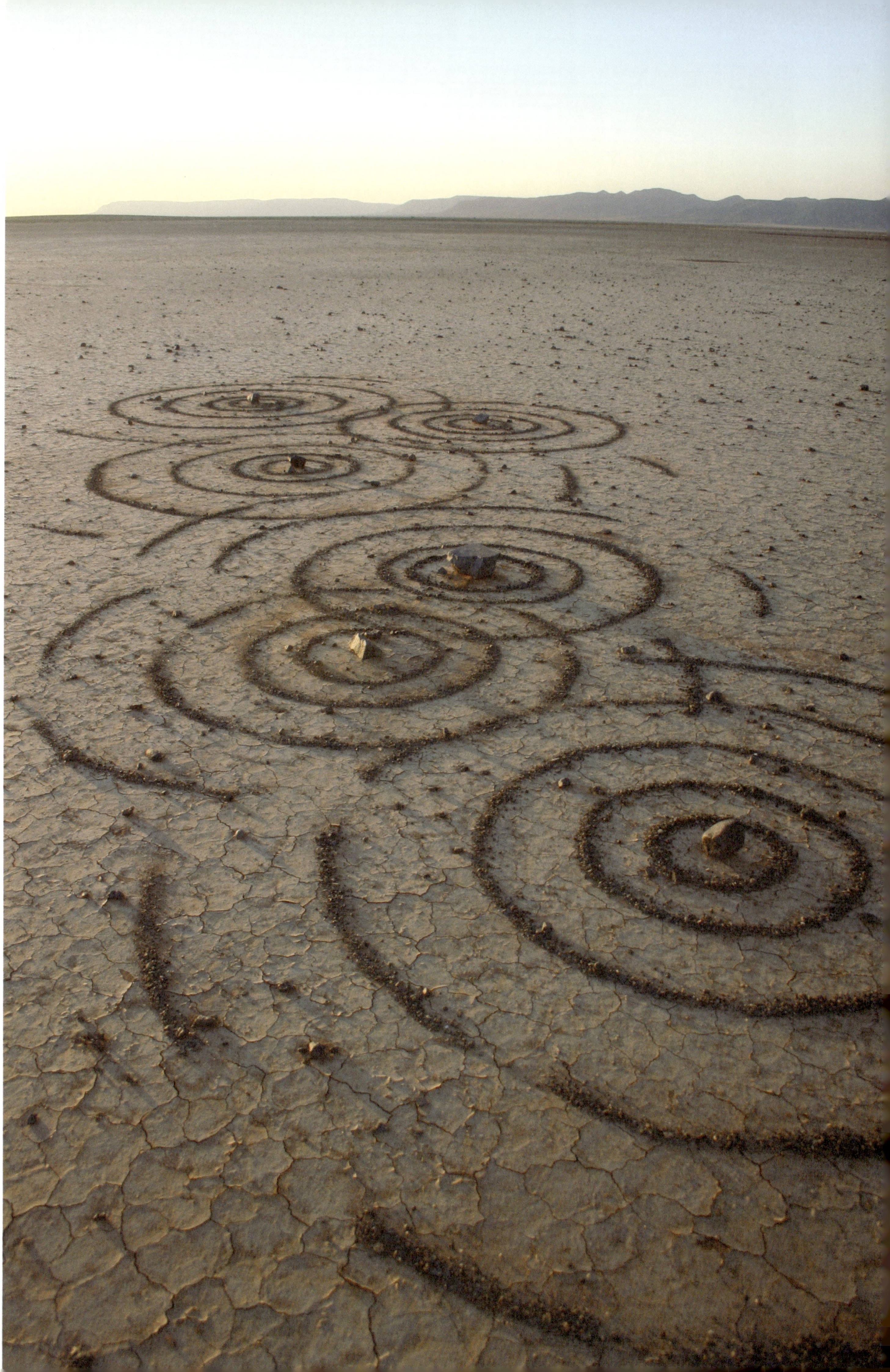

Interview with
David Southwood

The distinguishing feature of David Southwood's photographs, is his angle. Being shot by bullets made of rubbish, his interior series of township photographic studios, one-day flea markets, and enlarged scenic photography. At a glimpse, it does not look like he created anything, but through his viewfinder; he has taken a unique viewpoint of his subject. He has created an unusual atmosphere for each photographed portrait this time. With these photographs, the more you look, gradually the more you will fall under their charm.

David Southwoodの写真の特徴は、彼の視点そのものである。撃たれた弾丸の破片、タウンシップの写真店のインテリア・シリーズ、フリーマーケットの一日、広大な風景写真。一見、何でもないような設定が、彼のファインダーを通すことにより独自の視点で被写体がとらえられる。今回の彼のポートレート撮影も不思議な雰囲気を醸し出す一枚となった。見れば見るほどジワジワと魅せられてくる写真である。

David Southwood Profile

Born in Pietemarizburg in 1971, he obtained a BA in 1995, majoring in History and Legal Studies at the University of Natal. In 1996 he moved to Cape Town and in 1998 he worked as a photojournalist with the Sunday Times in Durban. Southwood's work can be found at the Finish Museum of Photography.

1971年、Pietemarizburg生まれのフォトグラファー。95年University of Natalにて歴史と法律の学士号を取得。その後ケープタウンへ移住し、98年ダーバンのSunday Timesにフォトジャーナリストとして勤務。Southwoodの作品はFinish Museum of Photographyに展示されている。

CASE-BULLETS

STUDIOS-DUMILE

STUDIO DS

MILNERTON FLEA MARKET
BIGLAND

BLUECHAIRS

FLASHGLASSES

FLASHMILNMAN

N1 HIGHWAY

N1 HIGHWAY

'African Salad' is a book that is getting a reputation for the documentation of everyday life. This is a book that compiles photographer Stan Engelbrecht's photographs of ordinary life, and writer Tamsen de Beer's interviews with families, from their visits to normal homes. This photographic compilation shows some of the author's favorite homes and homemade food from their experiences gained from visiting 60 families, which introduce residents with a variety of living of styles. This publication will be released in London, and is also scheduled to be released in other countries. We heard about Engelbrecht and Beer's plans for the release of 'African Salad' at a downtown café in Cape Town.

南アフリカの日常生活を記録した一冊の本「African Salad」が評判になっている。フォトグラファーのStan EngelbrechtとライターのTamsen de Beerが一般家庭を訪れ、普段の生活を撮影し、家族にインタビューをしてまとめたものである。60家庭のお気に入りの料理や家の外観、室内、住人の暮らしぶりが紹介され、まるで自分たちが南アフリカの多くの家庭に訪問して、生活の一部を体感している気持ちにさせてくれる写真集である。ロンドンでの発刊も決まり、今後各国で発行していく予定だそうだ。ケープタウンのダウンタウンのカフェでStanとTamsenに「African Salad」を発行する経緯などの話を聞いた。

Interview with
Stan Engelbrecht & Tamsen de Beer of Day One Publishing

Day One Publishing (Stan Engelbercht & Tamsen de Beer) Profile

Day One is a Cape Town-based mutual admiration society going as a publishing company. It came into being over a bottle of wine and a good photograph. Day One is Stan Engelbrecht, Stephan le Roux and Tamsen de Beer. They share a contemporary understanding of South African life and culture.
Stan Engelbrecht is a noted Cape Town-based photographer with a life-as-art approach to his subject matter. He travels between Cape Town and Johannesburg. Best known for The Caution Horses, this is his third book.
Stephan le Roux runs a television-branding company in Johannesburg. He is responsible for some of the most successful brands and branding exercises on television. He secretly dreams of becoming a playwright.
Tamsen de Beer has ten years experience as a media practitioner spanning print, broadcast and digital media. Writing is her first love and second nature. She has a four-year old boy and lives in Kalk Bay.

Day Oneはケープタウンに拠点を置く出版社。メンバーはStan Engellbrecht、Stephan le Roux、Tamsen de Beerの3人で、南アフリカの生活と文化を理解し合っている。
Stan Engellbrechtはケープタウンを代表する写真家のひとりで、生活をアートになぞらえた作風が特徴。ケープタウンとヨハネスブルグを行き来する。自身の3冊目の写真集『The Caution Horses』が最もよく知られている。
Stephan le Rouxはヨハネスブルグにあるテレビ番組企画会社を経営。最も人気のある番組や企画運営を担当する。そんな彼の密かな夢は脚本家になることである。
Tamsen de Beerは紙媒体全般、放送、デジタル・メディアに精通した業界人として10年のキャリアを持つ。書くことは彼女の初恋であり、第二の才能である。現在、4歳になる息子と共にKalk Bayに在住。

AFRICAN SALAD/ 2006/ DAY ONE PUBLISHING

+81: When did you start Day One?
Day One (DO): Day One Publishing was founded in 2004 by Stephan le Roux, Stan Engelbrecht and Tamsen de Beer.

+81: Please tell us the concept of African Salad and the story behind it.
DO: African Salad is a book about the real South Africa. We have the kind of flavor you just won't find anywhere else on the planet. We got to really thinking about what it meant to be at home. It came down to mom cooking your favorite meal for Sunday lunch with the family. Whoever we are in this country, food and family make us happy.

This book is very much a product of the process of finding real South African flavor. In total we knocked on about 120 doors right across the country. We approached certain houses rather than others because of how they looked - cared for, characterful, eccentric, typical of a period, lived-in.

Every family that contributed had a story to tell, and enjoyed the opportunity to tell it. Even those with the saddest stories knew how to laugh. Each recipe had a story too. Not only the story of its origin, but the memory of the many occasions on which the dish had been made, and of the loved ones - both grown up and departed - that had enjoyed them.

It was such a privilege for us to venture briefly into these many lives. These photographs of houses and the people who live in them are a document of contemporary South African family life. Their stories have given us a real sense of the flesh-and-blood people lined up behind the facts of our past.

+81: What do you think are the qualities of South African's publishing?
DO: It seems that South African book-makers have moved beyond the fact of our liberation to looking critically at the ordinary life of fictional or real characters going about the business of life. This is good news for South African publishing. Because increasingly, writers and publishers are producing works that smack of realness, of truth. There are more and more young start-up publishing companies. With the younger blood at the helm of more established publishing companies, bringing a fresh understanding of story and narrative and its place in South Africa. Although the book-buying market in this country remains tiny - a mere 3 to 4% of the population - there is an emerging appetite among a growing black middle-class for literature of all kinds.

Warden house LRG

Brixton portrait

Stan Engelbrecht & Tamsen de Beer of
Day One Publishing

+81: What do you feel about the environment of South Africa?
DO: The South Africans that have not left the country are committed to making it work. Black or white, those that have stayed, are here to stay. Economic disparity between the rich and the poor is the biggest problem. Mismanagement by the government of the delivery of basic services such as houses, running water, sanitation is also a big problem because it perpetuates poverty. Unemployment is a huge problem. But South Africans are talking about these problems and there is a communal goodwill in the country that wants to find solutions.

South Africa is a very beautiful country. Its peoples are beautiful, its geography, fauna and flaura are beautiful. There is still so much optimism even though the honeymoon period post-1994 has gone. The one thing that unites us all is our love of this country.

+81: What's your future vision?
DO: We propose a series of books documenting and preserving South African society and culture as we find it today - humble, optimistic, authentic, original. This is our vision: to find authentic South African flavour, nurture it, celebrate it, encourage it. Already we have franchised the African Salad concept and are in production on a similar book for the German market, with a German editorial team presently on the road looking for houses, families and recipes in Germany.

Our South African book is in its third reprint, and is due to be translated into German. There is a television series of the book in development with the South African Broadcast Corporation. We are in production on two new South African books, with another two in development. We aim to create a new genre of coffee-table books in South Africa : new Africana; out with the old sketches of wild animals by colonialist botanists; out with the collections of African bracelets and necklaces. In with the new Africana - contemporary, uniquely South African, with a global appeal.

+81：Day Oneを始めましたのはいつですか？
Day One（以下DO）：2004年にStan Engellbrecht、Stephan le Roux、Tamsen de Beerの3人で始めました。

+81：『African Salad』のコンセプトと背景を教えてください。
DO：本当の南アフリカの姿を表したのが『African Salad』。世界中どこを探しても見つからない唯一無二の本です。私たちは家にいることがどういうことを表すのかを真剣に考えるようになりました。それは日曜に家族と共に食べる、母親の手料理に繋がっていきます。食べ物と家族が、この国にいる全ての人を幸せにしてくれるのです。

この本は、本場の南アフリカ料理の作り方を紹介しています。全国各地、計120世帯を訪れました。普通の家ではなく、愛情に溢れ、特徴があり、風変わりで、時代を象徴するような人が住んでいるような家を取り上げるようにしました。どの家庭も物語があり、それを話す機会を楽しんでいました。一番悲しかった思い出さえも笑いに変えることができ、どのレシピにも物語がありました。そのレシピ誕生の話だけではなく、料理が作られるまでの様々な過程の思い出と、その家庭の中で成長していく人、そして去っていく人全ての愛が料理の中に詰まっているのです。

様々な生活を垣間みることが、私たちにとってとてもプラスになりました。写真に映し出された家やそこに住む人々は、現代における南アフリカの家庭生活のドキュメンタリーです。過去の事実に隠された生身の人々の本当の感覚を知ることができます。

+81：南アフリカの出版業の特徴について教えてください。
DO：南アフリカの出版社は、日常的なことも非日常的なことも自由に批判できるようになり、真実を一歩踏み込んだ形で表現しています。これは南アフリカの出版業にとってよいことです。ライターや出版社はリアルなものを作りだしています。そして、新しい出版社がたくさん増えてきました。若い人々のやる気が老舗出版社を先導し、物語に新鮮な考え方を組み込み国内での地位を確立します。我が国の本の購買市場はたったの3％〜4％と小規模ですが、黒人中流階級のあらゆる文学への欲求は高まっています。

+81：南アフリカの環境についてどう思いますか？
DO：南アフリカのように黒人と白人が共存し、明確な社会的意識を持ってそれを機能させようとしている国は他にないでしょう。富裕層と貧困層の格差が我が国の一番の問題です。政府による住宅、水道、衛生問題を含む基本サービスの誤った管理が、長年の貧困をもたらせた大きな原因です。失業率もまた深刻です。しかしながら、南アフリカの人々はそれらの問題から目を反らさず話し合い、国全体で解決策を見い出そうと努力しています。

また、南アフリカは美しい国です。人、大地、動物、植物が美しく生き生きと存在しています。1994年の民主主義化が終わってからも私たちは楽観的思考が残っているのです。そしてこの国に対する愛国心が私たちを結び付けているのです。

+81：将来のビジョンについて教えてください。
DO：私たちは、謙虚で楽観的、真正でオリジナリティ溢れる南アフリカの社会と文化を残すために、それらをシリーズ本にして記録していこうと計画しています。正真正銘の南アフリカ独自の味を育成、賞賛、奨励していくことが我々のヴィジョンです。African Saladのコンセプトをフランチャイズ化し、ドイツの市場に売り出すために現在同じ形態の本を制作中です。ドイツの編集プロダクションが、ドイツの家、家族、レシピのリサーチをしています。

当社が発行する南アフリカの本はドイツ語に翻訳され、3版目を増刷中です。South African Broadcast Corporationと組み、このシリーズ本のテレビ番組化も進めています。新たに2冊の南アフリカ・ブックを制作中で、他の2冊の発行も計画しています。また、植民地主義の植物学者による野生動物の古いスケッチや、アフリカのブレスレット、ネックレスのコレクションに関する大型豪華本など、新たなジャンルへの介入も狙っています。コンテンポラリーでユニークな南アフリカらしさを備えた新しい本を、世界に向けて発信していきたいですね。

Adelaide toni portrait

Durban portrait

Johannesburg

▲ ヨハネスブルグ近郊の金鉱山跡

Gold City Johannesburg

The one of the most dangerous cities in the world; dreaded Johannesburg. Certainly, out of all of the cities that I've been to so far, this town has the strongest scent of danger. However, it is here, that you will be captivated by a ceaseless fascination, rather than fear. Years ago, for those who had a dream of getting rich quick, this was Gold City, and people came here, from all over the world. After the end of the initial gold rush, things settled down for a while, then a new wave of people seeking fame and fortune, dreaming of gold, came from all over Africa.

In the 1960's New York's Soho, and East Village, was one of the most dangerous areas to be avoided. However, Andy Warhol, and young artists like Jean-Michel Basquiat, gathered in this dangerous area out of their own preference. The novelty and anxiousness of this danger, probably gave birth to an unusual aesthetic creativity, and to interactive work. Presently, Johannesburg is definitely still a dangerous town with many artists. Just like the 1960's, and the 1970's, in New York there was probably a feeling of fascination rather than fear of danger. This is a town that will make you want to visit again.

Johannesburg

NEW TOWN AREA_
Cityvarsity：デザインスクールがあり、近辺にはカフェやギャラリーもある。

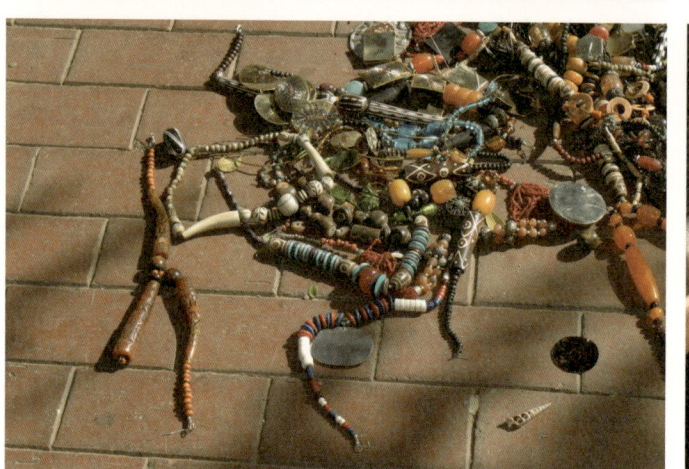

NEW TOWN AREA_
Market Theater：ライブ、コンサートから演劇まで開催されるMarket Theatreを中心に、広場では市場やカフェが並び、ヨハネスブルグの若者達の人気スポットとなっている。Africa Museumやギャラリーなども同じ敷地に併設されている。

ゴールドシティ ヨハネスブルグ

世界で最も危険な都市のひとつと恐れられるヨハネスブルグ。確かにいままでに訪れた都市の中では、最も危険な香りが漂う街である。しかし、恐ろしさ以上に惹き付けられる魅力が、ここにはある。昔、この街はゴールドシティとして一攫千金の夢を求めて、世界中からいろいろな人が集まってきた。黄金の山が終えたあと、しばらくは落ち着いていたこの街も新たな黄金の夢により、アフリカ中から富と名声を求めて、いろいろな人が集まってくる。

1960年代のNYのSOHOやEAST Villageは、最も危険な地域と避けられていた。しかし、アンディ・ウォホールやジャン・ミッシェル・バスキアらの若いアーティストは、この危険な地域に自ら好んで集まってきた。危険に対する緊張感と新しいものを生み出すクリエイティヴ感覚が、不思議と相互作用するのかも知れない。現代のヨハネスブルグは、まさしく危険で一杯なアーティストの街である。だからこそ60年代、70年代のNYのような、危ない以上の魅力を感じさせるのだろう。また訪れたくなる街である。

Johannesburg Night_ヨハネスブルグの夜
夜の時間帯人通りも少なく、外出することは危険というよりも無謀と言えるだろう。慣れない観光者であれば車で動くことも避けたい。

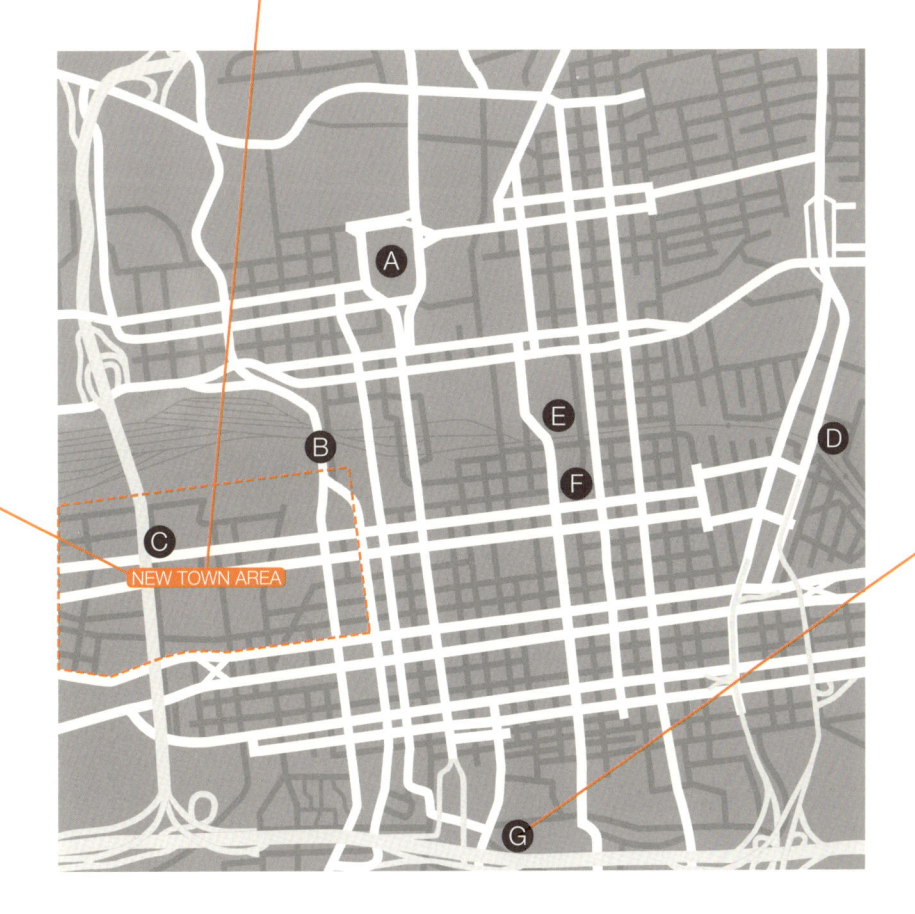

G_ Faraday Muti Market：動物の骨や乾燥草から、ビニールまでが伝統的な薬として扱われている。西洋医学でも東洋医学でも無いアフリカの漢方薬市場。

A_ Civic Center：Trinity Sessionのギャラリーは、B1Fにある。1Fでは、広々としたラウンジで飲食ができる。

B_ Nelson Mandela Bridge

C_ Africa Museum

D_ August House

E_ JHB Art Gallery

F_ Drill Hall

NEW TOWN AREA

087

Marcus Neustetter and Stephen Hobbs

+81: Please tell me about your activities.
Stephen Hobbs and Marcus Neustetter (H/N): A recent project by Hobbs/Neustetter: UrbaNET - Hillbrow/Dakar/Hillbrow manifested in an installation at the University of Johannesburg Gallery and as part of the group show THE COLOUR LINE at the Jack Shainman Gallery, New York. Curated by Odili Donald Odita.

+81: How about African remix conference?
H/N: The Trinity Session facilitated the Africa Remix Digital Africa Panel Discussion at the Johannesburg Art Gallery. The panel, made up of various experts from different disciplines and from different parts of Africa addressed challenges of local creative digital production in the arts, relationships to different industries and notions of networking through the digital medium. Artist presentations of technology-driven work, live reports from different African cities and interactive mobile phone messaging question and answer sessions all engaged the medium as effectively as possible, encouraging debate and stimulating ideas.

+81: What do you think of the quality of South African's design and art.
H/N: As most of the art projects are focused on a gallery-going audience, there does not seem to be enough interaction with a large majority of the local population that does not interact with the arts. The role of innovative and interesting cutting-edge design is starting to address this disparity through moving into the popular realm. The crossover between the two seems to start to address an interesting combination of intentions that allow audiences to be introduced to creative practice that is not alienating through the notions, debates and temples of art. While both the local art and design industry are quite small in comparison to the international scenes, the boundaries between the two are often not blurred enough for the industry to crossover on a regular basis.

+81: Can you tell us your future vision?
H/N: While there is not much funding support for cultural production in South Africa, the context forces a certain self-organizing innovative practice that allows designers and artists to look at generating means and support for themselves. This in turn implies more strategic and dedicated producers to make the effort and attempt to build an industry that does not only produce on the artistic platforms, but looks into other industries, virtual and public spaces for opportunities, networks, new audiences and support. This will develop a local cultural producer that understands his/her audience better and will be more savvy in how to position himself / herself and the work in both the South African and global context.

+81: あなた達の最近の活動について教えてください。
Stephen Hobbs and Marcus Neustetter (以下H/N): University of Johannesburg Galleryと、Odili Donald Oditaがキュレータションを務めたNYのJack Shainman Galleryのグループ展「THE COLOUR LINE」で、最新プロジェクト「UrbaNET - Hillbrow/Dakar/Hillbrow」のインスタレーションを行いました。

+81: アフリカン・リミックス会議はどうでしたか？
H/N: The Trinity Sessionは、Johannesburg Art Galleryで開催されたAfrica Remix Digital Africa Panel Discussionの手助けをしました。様々な分野と出身の各専門家たちが集まり、アート業界における創造的な地方デジタル産業、異なる産業との結びつき、デジタル・メディアにおけるネットワーク概念に取り組みました。テクノロジーを主に使用しているアーティストの作品、アフリカ各都市からの生中継やインタラクティヴな携帯電話メールによる質疑応答は、デジタル・メディアが討論を促しアイデアを刺激し合うツールとして有効であることを証明しました。

+81: 南アフリカにおけるデザインおよびアートの特性をどう思いますか？
H/N: ほとんどのアート・プロジェクトがギャラリー好きの人々に焦点が当てられているように、アートに関係ない大多数の地元住民との対話は十分ではありません。革新的で関心を引く斬新なデザインは、この人気を通して格差解決のための努力を始めています。このクロスオーバーは、アートの概念、討論、アートの殿堂を通してアートを身近に感じてもらえることを紹介するきっかけとして、興味深い組み合わせのように感じられます。地元のアートやデザイン産業は国際シーンに比べるとかなり小規模ですが、その産業が定期的にクロスオーバーするためには、二つの境界線が十分にぼやけていないのです。

+81: 将来のビジョンを教えてください。
H/N: 南アフリカには文化事業に対する十分な基金サポートがなく、デザイナーやアーティストは、彼ら自身で援助を見つけ出すという、独自で革新的な習慣を身につけています。これは、業界を作り上げようと努力している戦略的で献身的なプロデューサーが、アートの基盤を生むだけでなく、他の産業をみることによってヴァーチャル、公共スペース、ネットワーク、新たな観客とサポートの機会を得ていることを暗示しています。顧客をより理解したプロデューサーがローカル・カルチャーを発展させ、国内においてもグローバルにも、自分たちの立ち位置を見いだしていけるようになってほしいですね。

THE JOHANNESBURG CIVIC THEATRE

CIVIC THEATRE COLLIDOR

Johannesburg

The Trinity Session is a contemporary art production team that investigates the relationships between art and business, collaborative practice and network development. Hobbs' personal artistic interest is in the urban environment and public art interventions and Neustetter's in the electronic arts and growing virtual communities.

The Trinit SessionはアートとビジネS、共同業務とネットワーク開発の関係性を研究する現代アートのプロダクション。Hobbsは都市環境とパブリック・アートの市場介入、Neustetterは電子芸術と成長中のヴァーチャル・コミュニティに関心を持っている。

The pairing of Stephen Hobbs and Marcus Neustetter as an artistic collaboration fuses their interests in urban social change and virtual culture.
Over the years their artistic practice has resulted from experimentation with the juxtaposition of hi- and lo-tech, dead and new media interventions.
These experiments manifest in public space, galleries and museums and in the arena of their artist lab - the Trinity Session.
Taking into consideration the exclusivity of the museum and gallery context, current projects are focussed on social research and mobile platforms enabling their artistic expression.

Stephen HobbsとMarcus Neustetterによるアートユニットは、
都市社会の変化と文化に興味を抱いている。
長年に渡る彼らの芸術的手腕は、
ハイテクとローテク、新旧のメディアを並置した実験によって生み出されてきた。
これらの実験は公共スペース、ギャラリー、美術館、
彼らのスタジオThe Trinity Sessionで行なわれている。
美術館とギャラリーに特化してみると、進行中のプロジェクトは
社会調査と移動の場に焦点をあてたものであり、
それらが彼らのアート表現を可能にした。

Marcus Neustetter and Stephen Hobbs

ELAND

AFRICA REMIX
AFRICAN INTELLECTUALS CONFERENCE

Harry Penberthy

In order for the South African design industry to firmly take root,
City Varsity was established originating from design education.
Although they have only just started, their growth rate for the first batch stands at 100 pieces,
and since design from Johannesburg is widely recognized,
with this emerging talent they will be able to establish a design business.
They link to the hopes of the young people from Johannesburg.

南アフリカにデザイン産業を根ざすためには、デザイン教育からはじめようと設立されたのがCity Varsityである。
まだスタートしたばかりだが、第一期生100名が成長過程にあるヨハネスブルグにデザインの認識を広め、
デザイン・ビジネスを確立させる人材となるだろう。
ヨハネスブルグの若者たちの希望への架け橋となっている。

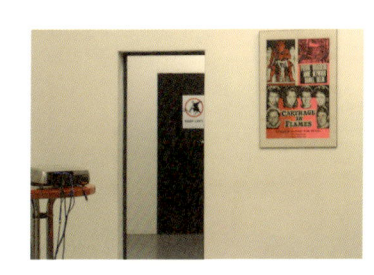

Johannesburg

Harry Penberthy
Principal City Varsity Newtown

James Bihl
Lead Animator Ontwerp

Hercules Maré
Technical Director CityVarsity

Anthony Dart
CEO / Lead Designer Ontwerp

The Trinity Session facilitated the opening of a new media school CityVarsity in Newtown, Johannesburg. Through network meeting, workshops, art interventions and school installations.The Trinity Session was able to position the school withing the current context and develop a conceptual backbone for the student programme. The first intake of 100 students at CityVarsity Newtown involved a two week orientation programme designed by the trinity session. Through various personal and group mapping projects, the students ventured into the city with a view to exploring the infrastructure of creative industries and cultural reseources within Newtown. As additional stimulus for the student body, the programmes, presentations, events and collaborative opportunities have been developed with local and international artists.

Trinity Sessionは、ヨハネスブルグのニュータウンにあるニューメディアの専門学校、City Varsityの開校を促進してきた。ネットワーク会議、ワークショップ、アートの導入、学校設備を通じて、最新の流行を把握し、コンセプトを持った授業を行う学校としてのポジションを確立した。City Varsityの第一期生100人は、Trinity Sessionが計画した2週間のオリエンテーションを受講。それは生徒が個人もしくはグループによる様々なマッピング・プロジェクトを行い、実際町に足を運んで、ニュータウンにおけるクリエイティヴ産業と文化資材のインフラについて考察するものだった。また、更に学生を鼓舞するため、国内外のアーティストによるプログラム、プレゼンテーション、イベントや共同制作の機会を設けている。

Harry Penberthy

Bie Venter / August House

Sixteen artists set up residence in a building called August House,
in inner city Johannesburg.
Bie Venter is the owner of this house inhabited by the artists.
Sought after able artists have gathered here, one after another to see her.
Naturally, she has a discerning eye for art.
Her studio with full of artworks shows it.
Let's introduce the residents of this talent-filled house in Johannesburg; August House.

16名のアーティストが住居を構えるヨハネスブルグ市内の「August House」ビル。
このアーティスト・ハウスのオーナーがBie Venterである。
ヨハネスブルグでは、彼女を慕って有能なアーティストが次々と集まってくる。
その見極める眼は、彼女のアトリエを見れば一目瞭然と言えるセンスの持ち主である。
彼女の眼にかなったアーティストは、当然ながら素晴らしい才能の持ち主が揃っている。
さあ、ヨハネスブルグの才能の館August Houseの住人を紹介していこう。

+81: What made you start managing the building?
Bie Venter(BV): One of the existing partners who has owned August House since it was built, liked our idea of converting it into loft and studio spaces and lent us the bulk of the money. Now that I am a partner in owning the building, I am making a garden on the roof for all the tenants to enjoy.

+81: What is the specialty of your building?
BV: Artists and cultural activity. We have at least sixteen professional artists living and working in the building, as well as an art gallery. Also the Art Deco style of the building is unique. It was built with love.

+81: Please tell us about creative attractions in South Africa.
BV: The Faraday Muti Market where traditional African muti (medicine) is being sold, which used to be an informal market under a highway flyover. The Joubert Park Project; a nonprofit institution organized by various artists and the Trinity Session; an art event, were contracted to utilize the land effectively as a public art space around about Faraday Muti Market. The Drill Hall is a heritage site opposite the Noord Street taxi rank very close to the Johannesburg Art Gallery, where the Joubert Park Project is based and has developed this old military headquarters as a cultural and educational tourism site, where creative projects are being hosted. It is also linked to the artist in residency program which is hosted at August House.

+81: Please figure out habitation in Johannesburg.
BV: It is as dispersed and transient as the inner city community, with people from all over Africa inhabiting buildings throughout the city. Traditionally, Newtown housed the mainstream of artists, but since property prices shot up, artists are looking for more affordable studio accommodation on the Eastern edge of the city.

+81: What is your plan for the future?
BV: I would like to create roof gardens on all the roofs of Johannesburg and work with artists to create safe playing facilities for children.

+81：このビルを管理するようになったきっかけは？
Bie Venter（以下BV）：August Houseの建設当時からのオーナーのひとりが、ビルをロフトやアトリエとして不動産活用するという私たちのアイデアを気に入ってくれて、資金の大半を貸してくれたのです。今では、私もオーナーのひとり。全てのテナントに喜んでもらえるように、屋上でガーデニングに励んでいます。

+81：このビルの特徴は何ですか？
BV：アーティストと文化活動です。ここには16人のアーティストを本業にする人々が暮らし、働いています。アート・ギャラリーもあります。それに、アール・デコ様式の建物がユニークでしょ。ここは愛で成り立っているのです。

+81：ヨハネスブルグのクリエイティヴ・シーンの特徴について教えて下さい。
BV：アフリカ黒人社会の伝統的な呪術医が調合した薬（植物や動物はもちろん、人体の一部までも薬剤になる）が入手できるFaraday Muti Marketという、もともとは高速道路の高架下にあった闇市。それが今、売りに出されているのです。そこで、アーティストにより結成された非営利団体Joubert Park Projectとアート・イベントのTrinity Sessionが、新たにFaraday Muti Market界隈をパブリックアートの活性の場とすることで使用契約しました。ヨハネスブルグ・アート・ギャラリーのすぐそばにあるNoord通りのタクシー乗り場の向かい側に位置するDrill Hallは文化遺産であり、Joubert Park Projectが本拠地を置いている場所でもあります。もともと軍用基地だったものをクリエイティヴ・プロジェクトが開催される、文化・教育を発信する観光地にまで発展させたのです。August Houseで行われているアーティストのための居住プログラムにもリンクしています。

+81：ヨハネスブルグのアーティストの住居について教えてください。
BV：アフリカ中から人々がやってきて街中に住んでいる都心部のコミュニティと一緒で、分散されて一時的なものかしら。昔から、Newtownにはメジャーなアーティストたちが居を構えているけど、物価が高騰した今、街の西のはずれに安いアトリエを探しているアーティストが目立ちますね。

+81：将来的なプランを教えてください。
BV：ヨハネスブルグ中の屋上という屋上をガーデニングで埋め尽くしたいです。あとは、子供の遊び場をアーティストと一緒に造りたいですね。

Johannesburg

In 1998, Bie Venter formed Bie cc, providing Logistical Assistance in Contemporary Art and Exhibitions. From her experience of exhibitions, Bie recognized the need for a fully comprehensive service dealing with the installation, specialized packing and shipping of materials, and has thus far put her talents to coordinating two Johannesburg Biennales.

Bie Venterは展覧会の運搬業務会社、「Bie cc」を1998年に設立。数多くの展覧会を手がけた経験から、インスタレーションを実施するには考え抜かれたサービスの必要性を認識する。以来、材料のパッキングやシッピングに特化したサービスを提供している。これまでに2回の「ヨハネスブルグ・ビエンナーレ」を主宰するなど、活動の輪を広げている。

Bié dealt with the installation of exhibitions like:
● "End of Time" by Jo Ractliffe - a gallery/ and site specific installation of billboards on the N9 in the Graaff Reinet, Nieu Bethesda district.
● "Memorias Intimas Marcas", an Angolan/ South African/ Cuban collaborative project under the direction of Fernando Alvim.
● "Marc Chagall – The Light of Origins" and "Joan Miro" exhibitions at the Standard Bank Gallery in 2000 and 2002.

Bie Venter / August House

Mbongeni Buthelezi

The power and dynamism of Mbongeni Buthelezi's artworks
will instinctively fixate your eyes on this spectacle.
If one looks closely at these artworks,
the colorful pattern makes you feel that the texture is familiar from somewhere.
He has created these artworks from unwanted, discarded material from everyday life.
In this atelier, the materials used for
this artwork are mainly an array of colored plastic discarded materials
which are covering whole surface instead of paints.
The canvases were constructed with stuck on color-tinted material, piece by piece.
The artworks have already received a great deal of world-wide attention
and recognition, which introduce Mbongeni Buthelezi as an ecology artist.

作品のダイナミックさと力強さに思わず目が釘づけになる。
作品をよく見ると、カラフルな絵柄にはどこか見慣れた質感を感じる。
そう、彼の作品は日常生活で捨てられる廃棄物を材料に作られているのだ。
アトリエには、アートワークの材料であるプラスチックを主体とした色とりどりのゴミ(?)が、
絵の具代わりに一面に敷きつめられている。
キャンバスに材料ひとつずつの色彩を確認し、貼りながら作っていく。
すでに作品も評価され、世界が最も注目するエコロジー・アーティスト
Mbongeni Butheleziを紹介する。

Johannesburg

Born in Johannesburg, 1965, he lived in a township, had no money and couldn't afford to buy any materials so he decided to produce works from what his daily environment had to offer: plastic wrappings of all kinds and sizes. He studied for a Teacher Training Course at Johannesburg Art Foundation before moving to the University of Witwatersrand. Lives and works in Johannesburg.

1965年、ヨハネスブルグ生まれ。タウンシップで暮らし、金銭的余裕がなかったため、日常生活の中で得られる様々な種類やサイズのビニール包装で作品を作るようになる。Johannesburg Art Foundationで教職課程を修了後、University of Witwatersrandで学ぶ。現在もヨハネスブルグにて活動中。

Mbongeni Buthelezi

Kudzanai Chiurai

Kudzanai Chiurai loves and respects Basquiat and his style is reminiscent of this,
with strong lines and diverse colors.
Hence, this charming work is a bold composition.
Chiurai, is a young artist with future promise, an artist who symbolizes new Africa,
and is recognized both internationally and domestically,
is the one of the first generation
after the birth of independent Zimbabwe, transformed from Rhodesia.
Wherever you look when you visit his atelier,
you will see the creation of a unique scene.

Kudzanai Chiuraiの作風は、本人も敬愛するという
バスキア（Basquiat）を彷彿させる力強いラインと色彩。
そして大胆な構図が魅力的な作品である。
Chiuraiは、ローデシアから独立してジンバブエに変わった後に生まれた最初の世代であり、
新しいアフリカを象徴するアーティストとして国内外から評価され、
今後を期待される若手アーティストである。
どこを見てもユニークな光景をかもしだす彼のアトリエを訪れた。

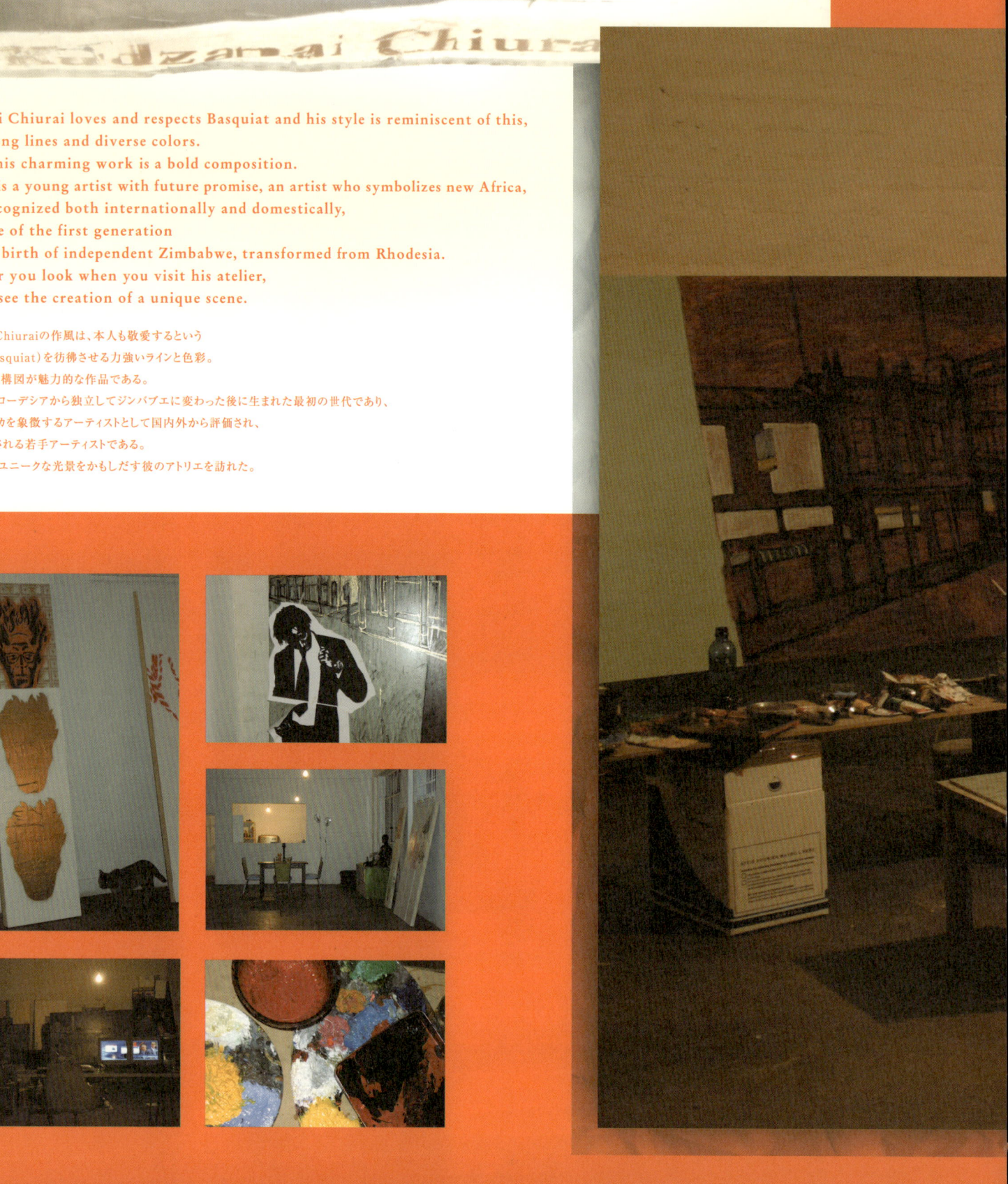

Johannesburg

Recent Exhibitions and Awards:
2005: Top 100 dazzlers and doers in South Africa, mail & guardian, South Africa
2004: Zuva Gallery, Johannesburg
2004: Brixton Art Gallery, London
2003: Most Promising Art Student, University of Pretoria
2000: Merit Award, National Gallery of Zimbabwe

Born in 1981 in Zimbabwe, Kudzanai Chiurai is an internationally acclaimed young artist now living and working in south africa. He was the first black student to graduate with a BA (fine art) from the University of Pretoria. Regarded as part of the "Born Free" generation in Zimbabwe because he was born one year after the country's independence from Britain.

1981年、ジンバブエ生まれ。南アフリカを拠点に活動する若手アーティストで、国際的にも高い評価を受けている。黒人として初めてUniversity of Pretoriaのファイン・アートの修士課程を修了。ジンバブエが英国から独立を果たした1年後に誕生した彼は、「Born Free」世代の一人として知られる。

Lawrence Lemaoana

This artwork, which has an intense impact, are instinctively funny,
and won the prestigious prize for excellence; the Absa L'Atelier award.
As for the background behind this artist, he was originally a rugby player,
and he says this was a huge influence for him.
Goal post is drawn at the far end of this artwork, and he wears a pair of rugby shoes.
A richly colored bunch of flowers and a blue sky,
a heavenly tablecloth and pink gown, you will think is gorgeous.
These are unforgettable colors. This is a young artist with a lot of future promise.

強烈なインパクトと思わず微笑んでしまうこの作品は、
2005年の南アフリカAbsa L'Atelier 賞の最優秀賞に輝いた。
アーティストとしての背景には、昔ラグビープレヤーだったことが大きく影響していると語る。
確かに作品の奥には、ラグビーのゴールポストが描かれ、作品に登場する彼本人はラグビーシューズを履いている。
そして、この極彩色の花畑と青空、
ピンクのガウンとテーブルクロスの天国を思わせる華やかさは、忘れられない色彩である。
今後が期待される若きアーティストだ。

+81: Please tell us background to your works.
Lawrence Lemaoana (LL): My work deals with the issues of South African Black masculinity. It started off with me being a rugby player. I realised that my identity in this sport was a major flaw, especially in South Africa where race issues are major subject. I started playing with colour as a tool, so I created an all black Rugby team, I designed the costume that each player wears, but the team is made up of just one person in different positions in the same constructed space. I then photographed these positions and assembled them on photoshop. I also make fabric collages, assembling feminised fabrics that speak of manhood.

+81: What does art mean to you?
LL: I have been told by one of my most respected lectures, David Paton, that the word art resides in the word artifice. Therefore art is bringing non-existent things into existence. It's essentially an all-encompassing experience of saying things in the most interesting ways.

+81: What do you feel about the environment of South Africa?
LL: It's an environment where new spaces are being created and old ones being are questioned, a lot more than ever before. I think the art world needs to be shaken to accommodate all people with talent. I think that black artists need to move from complacent victimhood to new and innovative spaces of creativity and that white artists need to open up their minds to accommodate them.

+81: 作品の背景について教えてください。
Lawrence Lemaoana (以下LL): 私の作品は、南アフリカの黒人の男らしさに関する問題をテーマにしています。それは自分自身がラグビーのプレーヤーだったことがきっかけになっています。ラグビーというスポーツにおける私のアイデンティティ（黒人がラグビーをするということ）は、特に人種問題という大きな問題を抱える南アフリカにおいて、大きなハンディであるということに気付きました。そこでまず考えたのが、私が黒人であるということを逆手に取って、黒人のみのラグビーチームを作り、プレーヤーが着用するコスチュームをデザインしました。ただ、このチームというのは私一人が1つの構図の中で様々なポーズを取っているだけなので、一つ一つのポーズを撮影し、フォトショップで合成しました。男性らしさを物語るために、あえて女性らしい生地を使ってコラージュを作りました。

+81: あなたにとってアートとは何ですか？
LL: 最も尊敬する教授 David Patonに、言葉のアートは言葉のあやの中に存在するのだと教えられました。したがってアートは、何もないところから、作り上げるということなのです。アートとは物事を面白く表現することそのものなのです。

+81: 南アフリカの環境についてどう思いますか？
LL: 古いものに疑問を抱き、新しい空間を作っていくという動きが今までよりもはるかに加速しています。才能のある人全てが、アートの世界を揺るがしていけるような環境を作る必要があります。黒人アーティスト達は、被害者だという現状に甘んじるのではなく、そこから新しいことや革新的なことに移行していかなければならないと思います。白人アーティスト達はどんどん心を開いて、和解していって欲しいですね。

THE DISCUSSION

Lawrence Lemaoana was born in Johannesburg in 1982. College in Johannesburg to study, and worked for three years towards a Diploma. After two years of working in the art industry on various projects, He is now back at university to study further for a degree. National Diploma in Fine Art at the Technikon of Witwatersrand 2005: Absa L'Atelier Art Prize winner.

1982年、ヨハネスブルグ生まれ。大学で学位を取得し、その後2年間で様々なアートプロジェクトを手がける。2005年にAbsa L'Atelier芸術賞を受賞。現在は大学に戻り、Witwatersrand工科大学にてファイン・アートの学位取得に向け、日下勉強中。

Lawrence Lemaoana

Gina Waldman

Gina is a two dimensional artist, since she is a co-entrepreneur of the fashion brand TWO.
You can see her bottomless creative power from the overwhelming number of her work.
Waldman has a lighthearted lively character, and her artworks have a unique worldly appearance,
combining subtlety and the splendidly powerful.
The very youthful work of Gina Waldman will attract attention in the future.

Ginaは、ファションブランドTWOの共同経営者であり、アーティストという2つの側面を持つ。
彼女のクリエイティヴ・パワーは、圧倒的な作品点数の多さでもわかるように留まることを知らない。
明るく陽気な性格のWaldmanの作品は、華やかさにパワフルさと繊細さを兼ね備えた、独特の世界観を持つ。
若さあふれる今後の彼女の活動に注目が集まる。

The exhibition "Shrines" show was at the Obert contemporary in Johannesburg, South Africa in 2006.

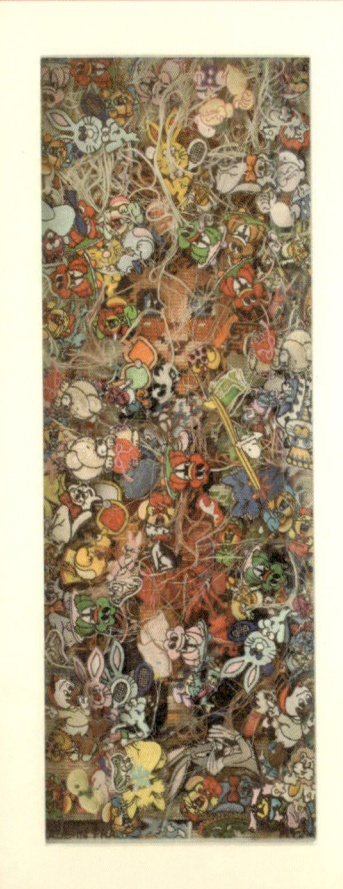

Woolworths in store art

Born in 1979, Waldman is a full-time artist who came through Wits University with a MA in Fine Arts. Her mixed media work explores notions of kitsch, excess, consumerism, taste and decorating. She also co-owns the fashion label TWO and is art editor of the JHBlive online magazine.

1979年生まれのWaldmanは、Wits Universityのファイン・アート科修士課程を修了後、フルタイム・アーティストとして活動中。彼女のミクスト・メディア・ワークはキッチュさや過剰、また消費者主義やセンス、装飾性といった概念を表現している。また、自身のファッション・レーベルTWOを展開し、ウェブ・マガジンJHBliveのアート・エディターも担当する。

+81: When did you start working as an artist?
Gina Waldman(GW): I had my first solo show as part of my master's degree in 2003. That show then developed into another show that was exhibited at the Standard Bank Gallery in 2004 and then the Bell Roberts Gallery (Cape Town).

+81: Please tell us the concept behind your works.
GW: Briefly, I look at kitsch, decorating and concepts of excess and I am influenced by popular culture, decorative objects and advertising.

+81: What does art mean to you?
GW: Art means different things to me at different moments in my life. At the moment art is something I am planning, thinking about, but it is in my head. I go through different processes. Perhaps in a month or two, I will be in art making phase.

+81: What do you feel about the environment of South Africa?
GW: South Africa is a diverse place. It is home, so it is safety, yet it is the most crime-ridden country in the world. It is full of the most beautiful things I have experienced, like Johannesburg rainstorms or the colourtul recycled craft objects, or the smell of the bush, but it is a country that has a lot of poverty and corruptions and illnesses like HIV/AIDS.

+81: What's your future vision?
GW: I am very interested in combining fashion and art. I own a fashion label called TWO, and we are currently showing at SA fashion week. It fits well with the conceptual threads in my work as I look at consumerism, perfection and excess, and fashion is about all these things.

+81: いつからアーティストとしての活動を始めたのですか？
Gina Waldman (以下GW)：最初の個展は、2003年に修士号の課程の一環として行ないました。その個展は2004年にStandard Bank Galleryで開催されたり、その後ケープタウンのBell Roberts Galleryへ巡回したりと、他の展覧会に繋がっていったのです。

+81: あなたの作品のコンセプトを教えて下さい。
GW：簡単に言うと、私はキッチュさや装飾性、過剰なコンセプトに注目しています。ポップ・カルチャーや装飾品、広告に影響を受けていますね。

+81: あなたにとってアートとは何ですか？
GW：アートは私の人生の異なるステップで、違った意味を持っています。今現在でいうなら、私が計画している何かであり、頭の中で考えているもの。私は様々なプロセスを通過していくの。多分、1、2ヶ月以内にはアート制作の局面を迎えるでしょう。

+81: 南アフリカの環境についてどう思いますか？
GW：南アフリカは多様性のある場所。ここは居心地のいい場所で安全であると同時に、世界で一番犯罪の多い国でもあります。ここは暴風雨やカラフルなリサイクル製品、木の茂みに香りなど、私が体験したとても美しいもので溢れているのです。だけど、多くの貧困や政治的腐敗、エイズなどの病気が蔓延している場所でもあります。

+81: 将来の夢は何ですか？
GW：ファッションとアートとの融合に興味を持っています。TWOというファッション・レーベルを自分で展開していて、現在は南アフリカ・ファッション・ウィークで発表しています。私のコンセプチュアルな洋服と、ファッションの特徴である消費者主義、完璧さや過剰さが上手くあっていると思いますね。

Lwazi Hlophe

The photographer, Lwazi Hlophe has continuously taken photographs of
life in Soweto for three years now, whilst taking photographs for a music magazine.
This time the Soweto visit could not happen without Hlophe as a guide.
The photographs that he continues to take of Soweto culture,
will be a valuable cultural record of South Africa in the near future.

音楽雑誌の写真を撮りながら、ソウェトの生活を3年間撮り続けている写真家Lwazi Hlophe。
今回のソウェト訪問には、Lwaziの案内なくしては行けなかった。
ソウェトという文化を撮り続ける彼の写真は、近い将来、貴重な南アフリカの文化記録として残るだろう。

fools hope world cup 2006 south africa.

The concept of my photography is simple really I ingage the viewer emotionally which is an influence from the old school photographers and the little things that life throws at us and we pass just cause see every day like the taxi picture that for me interests me. I'm also influenced by the impressionist painters Eg Edward Manet how they use light and how light always plays a huge part and how it distorsts things. Lastly I never plan how I'm go in to photograph my subjects I let them guide memy philosophy is "expose enough light for god to walk in and do his magic".

写真のコンセプトはとてもシンプルです。昔の巨匠写真家たちの影響もあってか、見る人をわくわくさせるようなものを目指しています。日常のささいな事、例えば、このタクシーの写真のように毎日の生活で目にするような物事に興味を抱いています。Edward Manetをはじめとする印象派画家の光の使い方、その光が果たす大きな役割、そして歪め方にも影響を受けています。被写体の撮り方を前もって計画することはありません。被写体が私を導いていくのです。「神のおはします所に照臨せば、奇跡あらん」というのが私の哲学ですね。

hands of a street gambler

Taxi

Born in 1979. Currently working as the main photographer for a South African music magazine which celebrates youth culture. Has exhibited at the Johannesburg Art Gallery and is currently working on a project called "I am music". He also runs a company called Brush Images Photography and is a growing brand.

1979年生まれ。現在、南アフリカのユースカルチャーに焦点をあてた音楽雑誌のフォトグラファーとして活躍中。Johannesburg Art Galleryで展覧会を開催している他、「I am music」というプロジェクトにも取り組んでいる。急成長を遂げるBrush Images Photographyの会社運営も行なう。

Lwazi Hlophe

Ephraim Molingoana

Ephraim Molingoana has a lot of talent and a varicolored career.
Born in Soweto, while living the life of a stylish model in London, he returned back to Johannesburg,
and he proceeded down the road of the fashion designer.
He tells us 'the most important thing is to believe in yourself, and knowing what you want to do in the future'.
In the future, he will verify this by cleaving a career by his own activity.

多彩なキャリアと才能を持つEphraim Molingoana。
ソウェト（SOWETO）で生まれ、ロンドンで華やかなモデル生活を送りながらもヨハネスブルグに戻り、ファッション・デザイナーの道を進む。
「最も大事なことは、自分自身を信じることと、将来何をしたいのかを知ることだ」と語る。
未来は自分自身で切り開くということを彼の行動が証明している。

+81: When did you start working as a fashion designer?
Ephraim Molingoana(EM): I started working as a designer in 2002.

+81: Please tell us the concept behind your collections.
EM: Most of the time I draw my concepts from the 50s and then modernize them and fuse them with our vast cultural diversity.

+81: What does Soweto mean to you?
EM: Soweto means a lot to me, I was born and bred there. Change in our country comes from there.

+81: What are you influenced by in South Africa?
EM: The struggle and the perseverance of my fellow country people, our rich diverse culture, our landscapes, food, the list is endless.

+81: How do you feel about the South African fashion scene?
EM: It's gaining a big momentum, We are going to be the next big thing after Europe.

+81: What's your future vision?
EM: Ephymol brand globally, that's the dream.

+81: いつからファッション・デザイナーとして活動を始めたのですか？
Ephraim Molingoana（以下EM）：2002年からデザイナーとして活動しています。

+81: ブランドのコンセプトを教えてください。
EM: 50年代からコンセプトを得ることがほとんど。それを現代風にアレンジし、南アフリカの膨大な文化の多様性と融合させていきます。

+81: ソウェトとはあなたにとって何を意味しますか？
EM: 私が生まれ育った場所でもあり、様々な意味を持っています。そしてこの国はソウェトから変化するのです。

+81: 南アフリカのどんなところに影響を受けていますか？
EM: 自国の人々が持つ努力と忍耐力、豊かで多様な文化、風景、食べ物など、言い尽くすことはできません。

+81: 南アフリカのファッション・シーンについてどう思いますか？
EM: とても勢いがあります。ヨーロッパの次に大きなファッション・シーンとなるでしょう。

+81: 将来の夢は何ですか？
EM: 夢はEphymolをグローバルに展開することですね。

Ephraim Molingoana was born in the early 70s in Soweto. After graduating from high school, he launched his modeling career in London, becoming the face of a worldwide Diesel Jeans campaign in 1996. He then returned to school to study advertising and

1970年初めソウェトに生まれる。高校卒業後、ロンドンでモデルとしてのキャリアをスタート。1996年、Diesel Jeansのワールド・キャンペーンのモデルに選ばれる。その後、学業に戻り広告とクリエイティヴ・ディレクションを学ぶ。現在は自身のファッション・ブランドを展開中。

SOWETO

Soweto, which is an abbreviation for South Western Township, is located 30 kilometers southwest of Johannesburg, and it is South Africa's largest township (a non-white residential area). The official population is 1.3 million. The 120 square kilometer expansive Hector Pieterson Memorial and Museum, and the old Mandela House, are also sight seeing places of interest on the tourist route.
Even within Soweto a gap exists between rich and poor, and at a glance some places seem wealthy, but at the back of these, there are many poor houses inhabited by struggling families. Presently, football stadiums, for the scheduled hosting of the 2010 World Cup, and railroads are under construction.

SowetoとはSouth Western Townshipの略で、ヨハネスブルグの南西30kmに位置する南アフリカ最大のタウンシップ（非白人居住区）である。公式人口130万人、120㎢の広大なエリアにヘクター・ピータソン記念館（Hector Pieterson Memorial and Museum）や旧マンデラ・ハウスなどの観光名所もあり、それらを巡る観光バス・ルートもある。ソウェット内でも貧富の差があり、一見すると豊かに見えるが、奥には貧しさに苦しむ家庭が多い。現在、2010年のワールドカップ開催予定のサッカー競技場と鉄道路線も建設中である。

Even today, parts of the world comes across racial prejudice.
Dividing humanity by only a difference in skin color is a mistaken ideology.
In the Republic of South Africa ten-odd years ago, this kind of prejudice
existed as a government policy.
The United Nations called apartheid "a crime against humanity".
Let's review how apartheid was fought, whilst heading down
a path of abolishment, and from when and
why this system began in South Africa.

現在でも世界の一部で見受けられる人種差別。
肌の色の違いだけで、同じ人間を分類するという誤った思想である。
南アフリカ共和国では、この差別が10数年前まで国の政策として定められていた。
国際連合から「人類に対する犯罪」とまで言われたアパルトヘイト。
南アフリカでは、いつから、なぜこの制度が始まり、
どう闘いながら廃止への道を歩んできたのかを検証してみよう。

Apartheid (a policy of racial segregation) was a policy of discriminating between whites and non-whites (blacks, Asians residents such as those from India, and those from mixed ethnic backgrounds known as coloreds) in the Republic of South Africa. The word Apartheid was introduced with the indigenous land law in 1913, however, institutional racial discrimination intensified from 1948 onwards, and became widely adopted. In those days, there were 4.9 million discriminating whites, compared to approximately 26 million people suffering discrimination. The South African government asserted that the "many races in South Africa who have their own language, and various different traditions and cultures, should develop independently. Apartheid is not discrimination, but a means of isolated development." However, behind this, whites aimed to secure cheap manpower, economic and political privileges, by treating blacks as migrant workers, robbing them of citizenship and a right to vote, and treating them as discriminators. As a result, this produced a variety of discriminatory laws. Specific examples of laws are given below.

[The Indigenous Land Law, and the Bantu Self-Government Promotion Law]
The South African government, made a large number of black groups migrate to a government created mini-state called the homeland, which was an area of land less than 13 percent of the entire country. The homeland was divided into 10 districts of separate ethnic groups, and the government planned to give each independent state autonomy. Despite the opposition from blacks, South Africa made the 4 homeland districts; Transkeian, Bophuthatswana, Venda, Ciskeian, independent from South Africa (from 1976 to 1981), however, this was not recognized internationally and was received huge criticism.

[Segregation Facility Reservation Law]
All public facilities; from restaurants to hotels, parks, transport, to public toilets, were distinguished for white and non-white use.

[Intermarriage Prohibition Law]
Marriage between men and women of different races was forbidden.

[Immorality Law]
Love relations by differing race were punished.

Like this, the policy of discrimination affected every part of daily life, as a countless number of laws were institutionalized.

However, there was also opposition from whites concerning these kinds of apartheid policies, and a full-scale movement by the black masses began. The African National Congress (ANC), the main group, which Nelson Mandela belonged to, and the South African Indian Congress (SAIC) took action against apartheid. From 1955 the ANC and SAIC, began to charged that "all people who live in South Africa, irrespective of white or black, belong", and a free charter was adopted, however, the government broke up gathering crowds, in the following year of 1956, and the leading activist, Mandela, was accused of high treason.

In 1976, a symbolic incident occurred. In the district of Johannesburg, Soweto, a riot centering on black students occurred, known as the Soweto uprising, resulting from the decision of the introduction of the use of Afrikaans by whites, in addition to English at school by governmental decree. Police forces trying to suppress crowds of black demonstrators clashed which became a gun battle, and approximately 500 civilians and more than about 200 students died, including a 13 year old youth, Hector Peterson. As a result of this incident, action against apartheid intensified more and more domestically, and criticism of the government of the Republic of South Africa from around the world grew, and international economic sanctions were imposed.

As a result, in September 1989 president Frederik Willem de Klerk was inaugurated, who advanced reform towards the abolition of apartheid and turned around policies. This governmental policy legitimized the South African Communist party, the PAC and the ANC, and Mandela was released unconditionally. In 1991, apartheid related laws decommissioned and apartheid was completely abolished. The European Community, thereafter the European Union, America, Japan, country after another, disbanded economic sanctions.

In April 1993, 26 political organizations joined a forum for multi-party negotiations, and in December of the same year the launch of an interim government was confirmed, and an interim constitution was enacted simultaneously. In April of the following year, the first all race participating general election was held and Mandela was elected president. During the same year, he acquired a seat on the United Nations General Assembly for the first time in 20 years, and once again joined the British Commonwealth of Nations, the Southern African Development Community (SADC) and the Organization of African Unity (OAU).

In addition, Mandela, made efforts to recover from the economic depression caused by economic sanctions, to get rid of the disparities between white and black under the system of apartheid, and called for cooperation and racial reconciliation. However, complete recovery from a shortage of manpower, financial resources, and a lag in the implementation of a development mechanism was not possible. However, in 1999 Thabo Mbeki, who was working as vice-president for the then Mandela government, anticipated a long-term strategy of state development, was inaugurated as the new president upon the wishes of succession from Mandela. Mbeki advocated an African Renaissance, and aimed to build a new leadership to carry toward the Africa. In fact, the South African economy after the inauguration, has grown markedly, and the rate of acceleration of economic growth is increasing as the hosting of the first football World Cup on the African Continent draws near in 2010.

Meanwhile at present the unemployment and crime rate are both high, AIDS is spreading, and the population of the townships (slum towns) are not decreasing. For South Africa, it is clear that the wounds from apartheid have not yet completely healed.

■ The Ministry of Foreign Affairs Homepage
■ 'SOWETO : A History" Philip Bonner, Lauren Segal, MASKEW MILLER LONGMAN 1998

アパルトヘイト（人種隔離政策）とは、南アフリカ共和国における白人と非白人（黒人、インドなどからのアジア系住民、カラードとよばれる混血民）とを差別する政策のことである。アパルトヘイトという言葉は、1913年、原住民土地法で登場するが、広く用いられるようになったのは人種差別を制度的に強化した48年以降である。当時、差別する側の白人は490万人に対して、差別される側は約2600万人であった。南アフリカ政府は、「それぞれ違う伝統や文化、言語を持ったたくさんの民族がいる南アフリカでは、個々の民族が独自に発展するべきだ。アパルトヘイトは差別ではなく、分離発展の手段である」と主張していた。しかしその裏には、黒人を差別者として扱い、市民権や参政権を奪い、出稼ぎ労働者として扱うことにより、白人による政治・経済の特権や安い労働力を確保する狙いがあった。そのための様々な差別法が生まれたのである。具体的な法律の一例として、下記が挙げられる。

【原住民土地法、バンツー自治促進法など】
南アフリカ政府は、国土面積の13%にすぎない土地にホームランドという「小国」を作り、多数派の黒人を移住させた。ホームランドは種族別で10地区に分かれ、それぞれに自治権を与え独立国にしようと政府は目論んでいた。黒人の反対にもかかわらずホームランドのトランスカイ、ボプツワナ、ベンダ、シスカイの4地区は南アフリカから独立（76年～81年）させられるが、国際的に認められずむしろ非難を浴びることになる。

【隔離施設留保法】
レストランからホテル、乗り物、公園に公衆トイレまで、全ての公共施設を白人用と非白人用とに区別した。

【雑婚禁止法】
人種の違う男女が結婚することを禁じた。

【背徳法】
異なる人種での恋愛関係を罰した。

このように、日常生活の隅々にわたる差別政策が、無数の法として制度化されていった。

しかし、そのようなアパルトヘイトの政策に対しては白人からも反発があり、本格的な黒人大衆運動が始まる。その主な団体としてネルソン・マンデラ（Nelson Mandela）が所属するアフリカ民族会議（ANC）、南アフリカ・インド人会議（SAIC）などが反アパルトヘイト運動を起こす。55年、ANCやSAICなどにより「南アフリカは、黒人、白人を問わず、そこに住む全ての人々に属する」という文言で始まる自由憲章が採択されるが、政府は集まった群衆を解散させ、翌56年にはマンデラなどの中心的な活動家を反逆罪で告訴した。

76年、象徴的な事件が起きる。政府の強制により、学校で英語に加えて白人が使用するアフリカーンス語の導入を決めたため、ヨハネスブルグ・ソウェト（Soweto）地区にて黒人学生たちを中心に暴動が起きた（ソウェト蜂起）。鎮圧しようとした警官隊と黒人デモ隊とが衝突を起こし銃撃戦となり、13歳の少年ヘクター・ピーターソン（Hector Petersen）を含め約200人以上の学生、さらに約500人の一般人が亡くなった。この事件をきっかけに、アパルトヘイト反対運動は、国内ではますます激化していき、世界からは南アフリカ共和国政府への非難が高まり、国際的な経済制裁を受けることになる。

その結果、89年9月に大統領に就任したフレデリック・ウィレム・デクラーク（Frederik Willem de Klerk）は方針転換をし、アパルトヘイト撤廃に向けての改革を進める。その政策方針によりANCやPAC、南アフリカ共産党を合法化し、無条件でマンデラを釈放。91年、アパルトヘイト関連法が撤廃され、アパルトヘイトは完全に廃止される。これを受けて欧州共同体EC（のちの欧州連合EU）、アメリカ、日本は次々と経済制裁を解除していく。

93年4月に26政党、組織が参加した多党交渉フォーラムで、暫定政府を同年12月に発足させることが決定し、同時に暫定憲法も制定された。翌94年4月には初めて全人種が参加した総選挙が行われ、マンデラが大統領に選ばれる。彼は同年中にアフリカ統一機構（OAU）及び南部アフリカ開発共同体（SADC）への加盟、英連邦への再加盟を果たし、国連総会の議席を20年振りに獲得した。

また、マンデラは民族和解・協調を呼びかけ、アパルトヘイト体制下での白人・黒人間の対立や格差をなくし、経済制裁による経済不況からの回復に努めた。だが、実施機構整備の遅れや財源・人材不足から完全回復することができなかった。しかし1999年、当時マンデラ政権の副大統領を務め、国家発展の長期的な戦略を期待されたタボ・ムベキ（Thabo Mbeki）が、マンデラの意志を引き継ぎ新大統領に就任。ムベキはアフリカン・ルネッサンスを提唱し、今後のアフリカを背負って立つニューリーダーと目されている。事実、就任以降の南アフリカの経済は著しく成長し、アフリカ大陸初の2010年のサッカーワールドカップ開催も近づき、経済成長は加速度を増している。

その一方で、現在も失業率、犯罪率は高く、エイズが蔓延し、タウンシップ（スラム街）人口も中々減少しない。南アフリカにおいて、アパルトヘイトによる傷は未だ完全には癒されていないと言えるだろう。

参考文献：
■ 外務省HP
■ 『SOWETO : A History』Philip Bonner, Lauren Segal, MASKEW MILLER LONGMAN 1998年

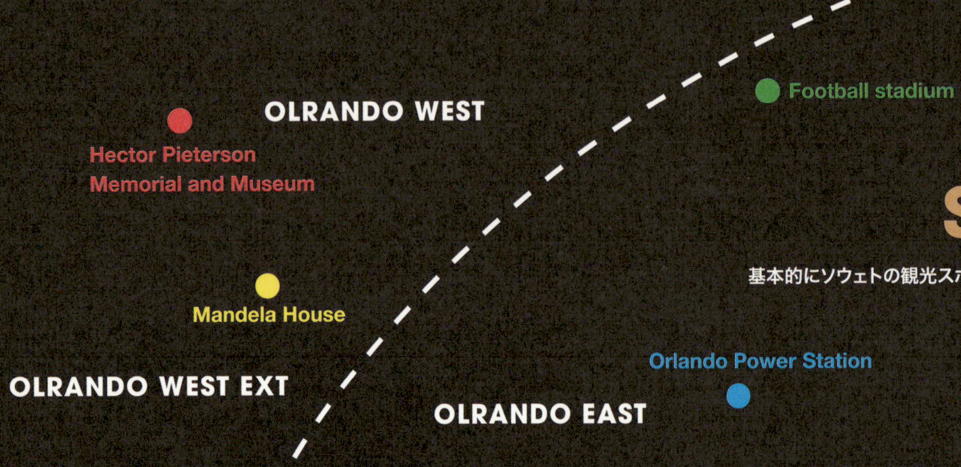

SOWETO map

基本的にソウェトの観光スポットは2カ所であり、交通の不便さからもツアーを勧める。

OLRANDO WEST
● Hector Pieterson Memorial and Museum

● Football stadium

● Mandela House

OLRANDO WEST EXT

OLRANDO EAST

● Orlando Power Station

● Hector Pieterson Memorial and Museum
ヘクターピータソン博物館

1976年ソウェトの学生達のデモに警察が発砲し、13歳の少年が犠牲となり、アパルトヘイト廃止へのきっかけとなった。この暴動の様子を写真と映像で記録として残している博物館。アパルトヘイト時代のソウェトの生活や文化なども映像で紹介されている貴重な資料館。南アフリカ・クリエイターの誰もが訪れることを勧める博物館。

● Football stadium
フットボールスタジアム

2010年のワールドカップのために建築中のスタジアム。近くに駅もできる予定で、交通も整備され、陸の孤島ソウェトも変わってくるだろう。

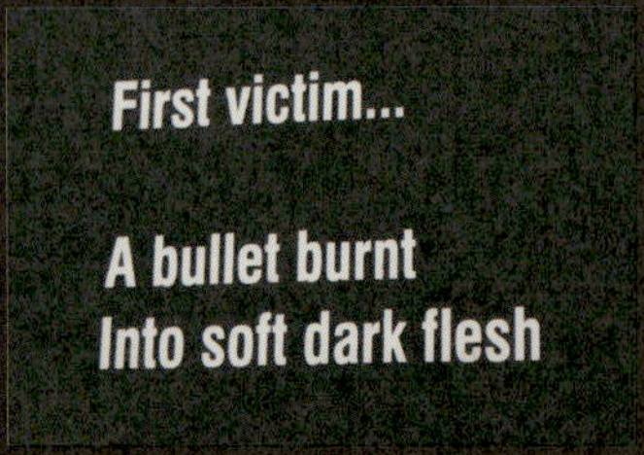

First victim...
A bullet burnt
Into soft dark flesh

● Orlando Power Station
オーランド発電所

● Mandela House
マンデラの家

1963年逮捕されるまで生活していた家。内部も有料で公開されている。リビング、子供の部屋、寝室、キッチンなど当時の模様を残した貴重な資料館となっており、本人の衣類なども保管されている。

JOHANNESBURG
SOWETO

CAPE TOWN

African Problem

The world has a variety of problems, such as global warming and the strain on resources. Come what may, we as humankind, have to prevent the onset of an awful crisis. The vital thing is to continue to voice concerns about various problems that will invite world destruction.

However, the problems occurring in Africa are not happening tomorrow, they are happening today. Although the near future is important, today, how do you feel when you are being confronted with people who are not looking towards the future, and are not understanding tomorrow and are losing their lives, right before your eyes?

+81 Ecode in this issue, with the theme, 'what can we do now?', will focus on the activities of Japanese in the land of Africa. We would like you to think about the energy of campaigning from people involved a remote distance away, to feel familiar with Africa, by understanding the existing situation in unknown Africa.

世界は、地球温暖化、資源枯渇などいろいろな問題を抱えている。私たちは人類が恐ろしい危機的状況を迎えることをどうしても防がなければならない。これらの地球滅亡を誘引する諸問題が大切なことは、今までも唱えてきた。

だが、アフリカで起きている問題は、明日ではなく、今なのだ。近い未来も大切だが、その未来を見ることもなく、明日を知ることもなく、今日、命を落として行く人たちの現実を目の前に突きつけられたとき、あなたは何を感じるだろう。

今回の+81 Ecodeは、「今、私は何ができるだろう」をテーマに様々なかたちで、アフリカの地で活動をしている日本人にフォーカスをあてた。見知らぬアフリカの現状を知ることにより、アフリカを身近に感じ、遠い距離を埋めた人たちの行動力について考えたい。

E:code
環境とデザインを考えるプロジェクト

What is the current situation for children around the world?
世界の子どもたちは、いまどのような状況なのでしょうか？

©UNICEF/HQ98-1100/Pirozzi

全世界で子どもは22億人いる。その2人に1人は貧困下（1日の生活費1～2ドル）で暮らしている。

2.2 billion children all over the world, one in two are live on less than US $1 a day.

年間1000万人以上の子どもが、予防可能な病気（肺炎、下痢、マラリアなど）により、5歳前に死亡している。

Nearly 10 million children die each year before their fifth birthday mostly from preventable causes.

エイズにより、1500万人の子どもが親を失っている。

15 million children currently have lost one or both parents to HIV/AIDS.

1億2600万人が児童労働に従事している。

126 million children are subjected to child labor.

What is UNICEF?
ユニセフ(Unicef)とは何？

©UNICEF/HQ95-0747/Balaguer

学校の募金活動を通じて誰もが知っているユニセフの名前。知っているつもりでもどのような機関で、どんな活動をしているかを理解している人は少ない。ユニセフについて調べてみよう。

Everybody knows the name UNICEF, from their school donation work. UNICEF is an organization that wants you to know about it, but few people know about what kind of activities UNICEF is doing.

正式名称は国際連合児童基金。1946年に創設され、第二次世界大戦後の悪環境におかれた子どもへの支援を始める。日本も1949年～62年まで支援（給食の粉ミルクなど）を受けていた。53年から開発途上国の子どもたちへの支援へと拡大し、現在150以上の国と地域で活動している。

ユニセフ活動の重点分野（2006－2009年中期計画）

1. 乳幼児への十分なケア
   子どもの生存と成長への支援（予防接種、栄養供給など）
2. すべての子どもが教育を受けられる活動
   基礎教育の普及と男女間格差の是正推進
3. エイズ問題への支援
4. 子どもを暴力、搾取、虐待から守る活動。予防と対策を支援
5. 子どもの権利を保護する活動

3つの指標（活動の優先順位指標）

☑ 5歳未満児の死亡率（1000人あたりの死亡数）　☑ 国民ひとりあたりの所得　☑ 子ども（18歳未満）の人口

活動資金

活動プログラムの支出は全世界で21億1900万USドル（2500億円）。活動資金は、政府による任意の拠出金が58％、民間募金割合が29％。日本の民間募金額（2006年）は、1.16億USドル（136億円）で、世界で最も多い。

1946 UNICEF is created by the United Nations to provide emergency aid to European children after World War II. 1953 UNICEF's mandate is expanded to benefit children in developing countries. Now in more than 150 countries and territories, UNICEF bring its influence to bear on the individuals and institution that serve the youngest generation.

Unicef Mid-Term Strategy Plan (2006-2009)
- Child survival and development
  Evidence-based child survival, nutrition and environmental interventions
- Basic education and gender equality
  Free compulsory quality education for all children
- HIV/AIDS and children
  Prevention, paediatric HIV/AIDS, parent-to-child transmission, orphaned children
- Child protection
  Protecting children from violence, exploitation and abuse
- Policy advocacy and partnerships
  Data, policy analysis, leveraging resources, child participation

Three indices (priority level index of activity)
- Under-5 mortality rate
- % of population below $1 a day
- Population: under 18

Donation Work
Total world activity program expenditure is 21.19 billion dollars (2500 billion yen). 58 percent of funding activities comes from voluntary government contributions, while 29 percent comes from private donations. The total for private donations from Japan in 2006, was 1.16 billion dollars (136 billion yen), a figure which is one of the highest in the world.

©UNICEF/NQ05-1987/Cranston

水と衛生 / WATER AND SANITATION

	U5MR 2004	都市 Urban	田舎 Rural	国の合計 Total
		Access to improved drinking-water sources(%) 2004		
West/Central Africa				
Mali	219	78	36	50
Nigeria	197	67	31	48
Eastern/Southern Africa				
Ethiopia	166	81	11	22
Kenya	120	83	46	61
South Africa	67	99	73	88
Middle East/North Africa				
Iraq	125	97	50	81
South Asia				
Afghanistan	257	63	31	39
Industrialized Countries				
Japan	4	100	100	100

※U5MR…1000人あたりの5歳未満死亡率

出典：THE STATE OF THE WORLD'S CHILDREN 2007

2007年の夏、ひとつのテレビ・コマーシャルが話題になった。Volvic (Danone Waters of Japan社)と日本ユニセフ協会との共同キャンペーン「1ℓ for 10ℓ (ワンリッター・フォー・テンリッター)」プログラム—アフリカの子どもたちに清潔で安全な水を—である。Volvicの水を1ℓ買うと、西アフリカのマリ共和国に清潔で安全な10ℓの水がうまれるという。水メーカーが売り上げの一部を水で困っている地域に寄付するという発想は、ミネラル水を購入する消費者にとっていつもの何気ない行動で、遠いアフリカ大地の人の水問題改善に貢献できるという喜びに変えた。しかも、1ℓ買えば10ℓ供給できるという具体的数字は、Volvicを飲んだ10倍の水がマリの役に立つと考えればわかりやすい。社会貢献を商品に連動した効果的なキャンペーンである。

In 2007 summer, one television commercial caught people's attention. Volvic and Japan Committee for UNICEF launched a joint initiative called "1L for 10L" program, to provide safe and clean water for the children in Africa. By purchasing one liter of Volvic water, ten liters of safe and clean water will be provided to Republic of Mali located in western Africa. A company owning a water brand is contributing to a region with water issues by donating portion of its sales. This concept has changed consumers' perception on their everyday action of purchasing mineral water to a pleasant feeling of helping water issues in a country faraway such as Africa. By clearly indicating that ten liters would be provided for every purchase of one liter, it is easy for people to understand that ten times the amount of Volvic you consume would become beneficial for the people in Mali. This program has been effective and successfully linked the product to the company's contribution to society.

「1ℓ for 10ℓ」プログラムプロジェクト責任者のキリンMCダノンウォーターズ株式会社の吉沢さんに聞く。

+81:"1ℓ for 10ℓ"プログラムは、どのようなことがきっかけで企画されたのでしょうか？
Volvic (以下V):ダノングループの飲料事業を展開するドイツの支社で発案され、ユニセフと共同で2005年にエチオピアを支援対象国として開始しました。翌年フランスで開始され、2007年に日本でも開始しました。ダノングループでは、各国の独自性を尊重しながら、良いものはグループで共有する社風があり、事業と社会貢献の両立という企業理念にも適合していたので、この企画に各国支社が賛同したのです。

+81:具体的に"1ℓ for 10ℓ"とはどのような流れで10ℓになるのですか？
V:Volvicの売上の一部をダノングループからユニセフに寄付します。この支援金額でユニセフがアフリカに井戸を作り、10年間のメンテナンスを行います。つまり安全で清潔な水を10年間供給する仕組みを作ることなのです。「単年だけでなく複数年に渡りこのプロジェクトを続けて行く」という意思のもと展開している、持続性を重視した支援なのです。もちろん私たちもユニセフと一緒にマリまで状況視察に行きました。

+81:現在までのキャンペーン結果や貢献実績などを教えてください。
V:まず、マリに延べ約7億ℓ供給されることを目標にしています。この数字は、1万人の人々に10年間安全で清潔な水を供給できる量です。支援金は、20本の新しい井戸の建設、壊れて使用できない井戸60本の修復、さらに地元の人々へのメンテナンスに関するトレーニングに充てられ、これにより、10年間維持する仕組みができます。7月2日から9月30日までのキャンペーンで、達成できそうな勢いです。

+81:苦労したこと、難しかったことはありますか？
V:キャンペーンの意図を正確に伝えられるかコミュニケーションの問題で悩みました。重苦しい表現だと違うと感じましたし、伝え方を誤ると、脅迫的もしくは偽善的な印象を与えてしまう危険性もありました。有識者の方々のご意見も参考にさせていただきながら方向性を決めてきたのですが、Volvicが成功しないと次に続く企業が難しくなるから成功して欲しいと励まされ、それが逆にプレッシャーでしたね(笑)。

+81:今後の展開スケジュールなどを教えてください。
V:2008年以降も継続的な展開を考えています。個人的にはマリの村にもう一度出かけて、子供たちの笑顔を見たいですね。そして、その成果をプログラムに賛同してくださった日本の消費者の皆様にきちんと報告したいです。

1ℓ for 10ℓ

Photo by hisashi okamoto

今までの旧式井戸 ▲

新しく作られたポンプのある井戸 ▲

かつて、マリは14世紀頃サハラ交易の中心地であり「黄金のマリ帝国」として、欧州でも知れ渡るほど繁栄していた。

マリ共和国の世界遺産「ジェンネ」は1280年頃に建てられた壮麗な泥塗りのモスク。1988年、世界遺産に認定される。

COUNTRY INFORMATION	
国名	マリ共和国
面積	124.1万km²
人口	1,390万人
首都	バマコ
民族	バンバラ族、プル族、マリンケ族、トゥアレグ族など23民族以上
言語	フランス語（公用語）、バンバラ語等
宗教	イスラム教、伝統宗教、キリスト教
独立記念日	1960年9月22日

地球人口の約1/6の10億人が安全で清潔な水を確保できていない

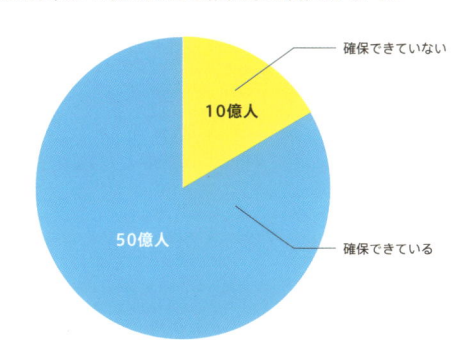

- 10億人 — 確保できていない
- 50億人 — 確保できている

地球人口の4億人の子どもたちは水に色がついていると思っている

- 4億人 — 水に色がついていると思っている
- 22億人 — 思っていない

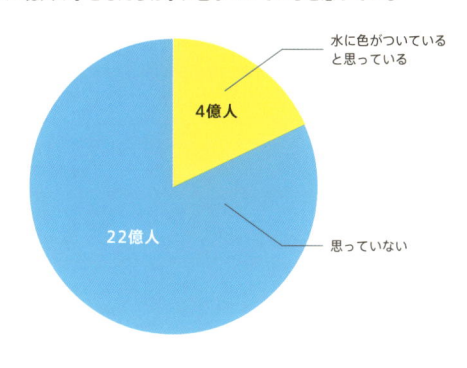

日本ユニセフ協会の浦上綾子さんに聞く。

+81：世界の水の状況はどのようになっていますか？
UNICEF（以下U）：世界全体で5歳未満の子どもが毎日4100人、清潔で安全な水や衛生設備の欠如により、下痢などの水に関係する病気で亡くなっています。また、地球人口の約6分の1の10億人が安全で清潔な水を確保できず、4億人の子どもたちは水には色がついていると思っています。つまり、透明な水を使うことのできない生活を送っているのです。特に、アフリカと南アジアの状況は厳しいです。地面に掘った穴からくみ上げた泥水、池や沼の水を飲まざるをえず、下痢やコレラ、寄生虫病などに苦しんでいます。水の質に加え、水源へのアクセスも、大きな問題です。自宅のそばに水源がなければ、日に何度も遠くまで水汲みに行かなくてはいけません。子どもたちは学校に通う時間がなくなってしまうなど、生活に様々な影響を与えます。

+81：今回の「1ℓ for 10ℓ」についての反響はありますか？
U：私たちにも、多くの反響が寄せられました。「このTV CMを通じて、ユニセフが水の分野でも支援事業を行っていると知りました」「水のビジネスを行っているダノン（Volvic）による支援に、とても共感しました」などの声もいただきました。"1ℓ for 10ℓ"の反響もあるのか、他の企業様からもユニセフへの支援を検討したい、とのお問い合わせをいただいています。

+81：支援プログラムは、マリでは開始されているのでしょうか？
U："1ℓ for 10ℓ"スタートに先立ち、ダノン（Volvic）にご寄付をいただき、プロジェクトを開始し、井戸の建設や修理を行っています。井戸の建設予定地に住んでいる女性は、井戸ができれば、作物を育てて食べられるようになる。農作物を市場で売ってお金も得られるし、水汲みにかかる時間が減り、子どもが学校に通えるようになるかもしれない、と嬉しそうに話してくれました。今後の活動では、住民たちが持続的に井戸を使用できるようメンテナンスのトレーニングを行い、また、衛生習慣の定着を図っていくことになります。

+81：今後の課題などがあれば教えてください。
U：サハラ砂漠より南のアフリカでは、子どもの死亡率が高く、水をはじめとする子どもの生存を守るための活動がとても重要です。その一方、近年、HIV/AIDSも子どもたちを取り巻く大きな問題となっています。毎分ひとり、15歳未満の子どもがAIDSで命を落とし、1500万人以上の子どもがAIDSで親を失っています。ユニセフは、HIV母子感染の予防や、感染した子どもたちの治療、若者への予防、子どもたちの保護などに取り組んでいます。皆さんに関心を持っていただきたい問題です。

マリの民族衣装  ▲　　一行を歓迎する踊り  ▲　　古い水汲みのスタイル ▲

AIDS in Africa アフリカのエイズ

参考資料 / Reference materials
DATA -debt AIDS trade Africa- website
UNAIDS website

Approximately ten percent of the world's population is living in the Sub-Saharan African continent. The reality is that the ratio of the number of people infected with AIDS accounts for over 60 percent in the world.

サハラ以南のアフリカ大陸には世界人口の約10％が居住している。AIDS感染者数比率は世界の60％以上を占めているという現実がある。

-UNAIDS

サハラ以南のアフリカは70％の人々が1日2ドル以下で暮らし、2億人が食に飢えている貧困状態にある。不良国債、AIDS、先進国とのアンフェアな取引というトリプルの危機によって、学校や病院の建設遅れ、労働者の減少、貧困から抜け出せない状況を引き起こしている。そうした状況から教育の遅れ、医者の不足、財政難、女性差別、AIDSに対する偏見などを生みだし、更なる感染者を増やしているのだ。母子感染に関しては、98％が未然に防げるものだが貧困や知識不足、偏見への恐れからAIDSであることを隠したまま出産をするケースが多いという。

EPIDEMIC OF AIDS
アフリカはAIDSウィルスによって世界に類をみない悲劇を生んでいる地域だ。25年前にAIDSが発見されて以来、現在1,700万人以上のアフリカ人が過去にAIDSで亡くなり、約2,500万人が感染。感染したうちの約200万人は15歳以下の子供である。毎日5,500人がAIDSで死亡、7,700人が新たに感染、そして1,400人の新生児は生まれながらにAIDS保有者だ。2006年に関しては、AIDS死亡者数は世界比率の72％にあたる210万人で、新たに世界比率の65％にあたる280万人が感染した。AIDS孤児は1,200万人にものぼり、2010年までに1,800万人まで膨れ上がる見込みである。

LIFE EXPECTANCY IN SUB-SAHARAN AFRICA
またAIDSによる短命化も深刻だ。ボツワナの1990年の平均寿命は65歳だったのに対し、2005年にはなんと約半分の34歳にまで縮まっている。AIDS成人感染率が世界第1位の33.4％を記録するスワジランドに関しては、1990年に57歳だったのが現在では30歳まで落ち込んだ。

だが悲観してばかりはいられない。ケニア、ウガンダ、ジンバブエではここ数年で感染者数の減少がみられる。これは世界基金などによるプログラムが功を奏し出した結果だ。ARV（抗レトロウィルス）を投与することによって延命治療が可能になる。アフリカにおけるARVの提供数は、2002年は5万件と感染者の1％しか行き渡っていなかったのだが、2006年には130万件の28％と大きな進歩がみられる。とは言うものの、残りの70％以上の患者が現在も薬の不足から死に直面しており、特に妊娠中の女性や子供への提供が急がれている。さらに、G8では2006年に"AIDS-free generation in Africa"を打ち出し、アフリカでのAIDS撲滅に本格的に乗り出した。2010年までに全てのAIDS患者に必要な治療と薬を提供し、AIDS孤児やサポートが必要な患者たちには適切な援助が受けられることを目標とする。そのためには、200〜230億ドルの年間予算が必要であるとUNAIDSは見積もりを出した。国際理解と基金援助が緊急に求められている。

サハラ以南のアフリカの生活費
70% ▶ **2**ドル以下

AIDS死亡者数 **1,700万人**
感染者数 **2,500万人**
1990-2006

1日のAIDS死亡者数 **5,500人**
1日のAIDS感染者数 **7,700人**

各国の平均寿命の推移（1990年 ▶ 2005年）
ボツワナ **65才** ▶ **34才**
スワジランド **57才** ▶ **30才**

In Sub-Saharan Africa two billion people are in a state of poverty and hunger, and 70 percent of people live on less than two dollars per day. The triple crisis of bad government loans, AIDS, unfair trading by developed countries is causing a state of perpetual poverty, a decline in labor, and a lag in the construction of hospitals and schools. From this situation, infected people are further increasing, producing stereotypes of AIDS, discrimination against women, financial difficulties, a shortage of doctors, lagging education. Concerning mother to child infection, it is thought that there are many cases of birth whilst AIDS is kept concealed because of the AIDS discrimination, poverty and a lack of knowledge, although 98 percent of these cases can be prevented.

EPIDEMIC OF AIDS
Africa is a region where the AIDS virus has produced an unparalleled world tragedy. Since AIDS was discovered 25 years ago, over 17 million Africans have died of AIDS to date, and approximately 25 million are infected and from this figure, two million are children below the age of 15. Everyday 5,500 people die of AIDS, there are 7,700 newly infected people, and 1,400 babies are born as AIDS carriers. In 2006, the number of AIDS deaths in Africa in terms of a world scale was 72 percent, or 2.1 million, and the number of newly infected on a world scale was 65 percent, or 2.8 million. The numbers of AIDS orphans are 12 million and to rise to 18 million by 2010.

LIFE EXPECTANCY IN SUB-SAHARAN AFRICA
Moreover, shortened lives from AIDS is severe. In Botswana in 1990, the average lifespan was 65 years old, compared to a dramatic decrease in 2005 to approximately half, 34 year in age. Swaziland has recorded the highest ratio of adult AIDS infected in the world at 33.4 percent, and at present, the average lifespan has dropped to 30 years from 57 years in 1990.

However, we cannot despair. Over the last few years, a decline in infected numbers has been seen in Kenya, Uganda, and Zimbabwe. This is from the successful results of a program of world funding. By administering ARV treatment (anti-retrovirus) it has become possible to prolong life. The number of ARV treatment provided to Africa, in 2002 was only 50,000 cases, or one percent of infected patients, however, in 2006 enormous progress were observed such that 1.3 million cases, or 28 percent of infected patients received ARV treatment. Having said that, over 70 percent of the remaining patients at present face death from a lack medicine, especially pregnant women and children where providing treatment is urgent. Furthermore, the G8 summit in 2006, came up with an "AIDS-free generation in Africa" and launched an all-out eradication of AIDS in Africa. It is aimed for by 2010, for AIDS orphans and those patients who need support to receive appropriate assistance, and to provide all AIDS patients with essential treatment and medicine. In order for this, the UNAIDS released an estimate of an essential yearly budget of 200-230 billion dollars.

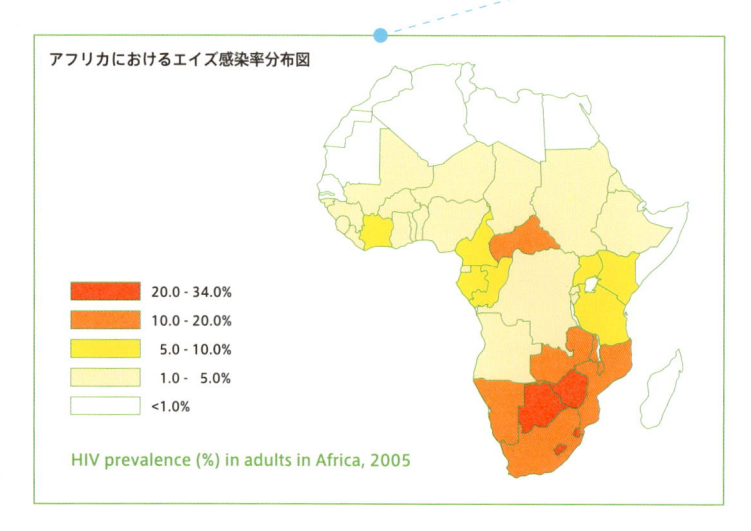

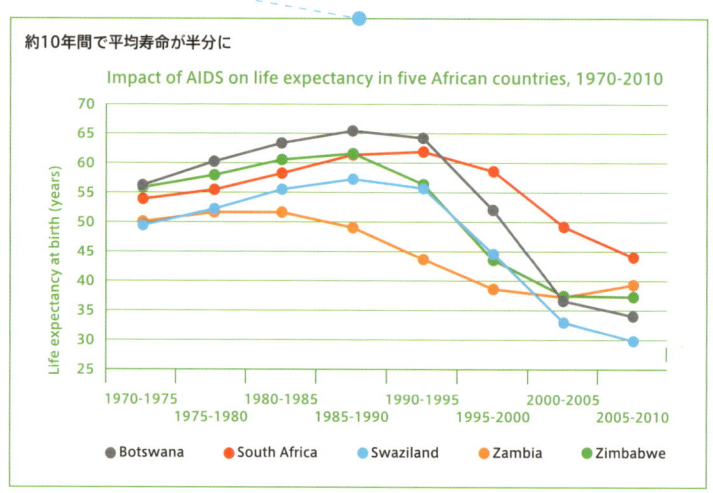

アフリカにおけるエイズ感染率分布図

- 20.0 - 34.0%
- 10.0 - 20.0%
- 5.0 - 10.0%
- 1.0 - 5.0%
- <1.0%

HIV prevalence (%) in adults in Africa, 2005

約10年間で平均寿命が半分に

Impact of AIDS on life expectancy in five African countries, 1970-2010

● Botswana ● South Africa ● Swaziland ● Zambia ● Zimbabwe

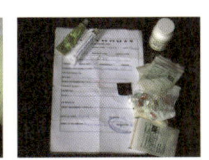

Noriko Asano is an expert on Africa, and she has visited more than 30 times over thirteen years. She introduced for us, the present situation for the country she is most interested in. What is happening in Malawi, and with an understanding of the present situation, what is best to be done?

At the African JAG Project, we first started volunteering in Malawi in the drought of 2004. Under a situation without food, adult workers, between 20 and 40 years of age, were not able to work, due to the spread of AIDS, and children, who would work in the fields, would not attend school. However, some time later we began to hear the news, that even with child labor, getting food had become difficult.

Even amongst a variety of African nations, Malawi has good public safety, and I think, this a really good country, since people are gentle and mild mannered. Probably tourists visiting Malawi, do not see real life, but leave with the impression that 'this is a good country'. However, the reality of the present situation in Malawi, is actually very severe. The spread of AIDS in particular, has cast a large shadow over this country. In addition, state-run hospitals number approximately 60, while overseas NGOs, and churches running private hospitals numbers approximately 30. Only approximately 90 domestic hospitals exist. Since the present government came in to office, there is free distribution of medicine, and a free offer of blood tests for those that can make it to a hospital. However, because there is a shortage of hospitals, those far away, as much as 300 kilometers, manage to come by road with car. And also, those that can come represent only a tiny fraction. Paying for expensive transportation fees, on one dollar a day living, for many people in this country is impossible. As a result, many people cannot go to hospital, and cannot even get medicine, are just bedridden, dying in terrible pain. Most are between 20 and 40 years of age. From our investigations, we found that the majority have lost their partners due to AIDS two or three years before, and are in the transition from stage three to stage four of the disease. Living without medicine, death will certainly visit in a very short space of time. In one village, more than 25 percent are HIV positive, which is not rare. Therefore, there are many bedridden people, and they know that they have AIDS. They just wait for death to come.

Here, let us go through some of the resulting problems again. One of the problems, are children who lose their parents, become orphans. A large number of these orphans, have contracted the AIDS virus from their mother during birth. The number of orphanages doesn't suffice at all. This casts a dark shadow over the future of children.

At present, our African JAG Project, we carry out VCT (HIV blood tests) in village areas without hospitals, we distribute transport coupons to state-run hospitals, and free treatment coupons to private hospitals, and give food aid to orphanages. With recent high-efficacy AIDS drugs, medicine given to those in stage three of the disease who cannot walk, are able to walk again if they are fed, and work is then a possibility. If this is the case, there will not be a dramatic increase in the number of orphans. Therefore, going to the hospital right away, and taking medicine is vital.
The smile of African children is something special. In midst of a situation, without money, or even water, the smiling faces of these children are the only 'glow'. In order to keep this 'glow', and to save even one child, we want you to know about the reality of this situation.
Therefore, we would like you to start doing whatever you can now, because we are simultaneously living life on the same planet!

Text by Noriko Asano
DJ Krush and the artist Sawada Jun, leading with their production of Es fun Es, work as a creators in the field of art, music, film, writing and photography. In the African Jag Project, they went around Africa on their own, energetically doing volunteer work. From 1994, they visited a total of 12 African countries approximately 30 times, and after visiting Malawi for the first time in April of 2006, this is already their third stay.

The Realities of MALAWI
マラウイの現実

13年間で30回もアフリカを訪れたアフリカ通の浅野典子さんに、今、最も関心のある国の現状を紹介してもらった。マラウイでは、何が起きているのだろう。そして、この現実を知ってどうすればよいのだろう。

私達African JAG Projectがマラウイの支援を始めたのは、かんばつが起こった2004年。食料がない上、働き手である20代〜40代の大人がAIDSの蔓延により働くことが出来なくなり、子供たちが学校を休んで畑を作っている。しかし子供たちの労働力では、今後、食糧確保が難しくなってくる…というニュースを聞いたことに始まった。

マラウイはアフリカ諸国の中でも治安も良く、人々も温和で本当に良い国だと思う。たぶん観光でマラウイを訪れても実際の人々の生活を見ない限り「いい国だね〜。」で終わってしまうだろう。
しかし、実際のマラウイの現実は、実に厳しいものがある。特にAIDSの蔓延がこの国に大きな影を落としている。また、この国には国営の病院が約60、海外のNGOや教会が運営するプライベート・ホスピタルが約30、国内に約90の病院しか存在していない。現在の政府になってから、病院までたどり着けば、血液検査、薬などは無料で配布されるようになった。しかし、病院そのものが不足しているため、遠い人では約300kmの道のりを車に揺られてやって来るのだそうだ。しかも、それを出来るのはごくわずかな人たちに限られている。一日1ドル以下で生活しているこの国の多くの人たちにとって、高額な交通費を支払うことは不可能だ。そのため、多くの人たちが病院にも行けず、薬を飲むことさえできず、ただただ自宅の部屋で寝たきりになり、苦しんで死んでいく。その多くは20歳代〜40歳代。私達が調査したところによると大半が既に2年〜3年前に伴侶をAIDSで亡くしており、自身もステージ3からステージ4に移行しているという。このまま薬も飲まずにいれば近い将来"死"が訪れることは間違いない。一つの村で25％以上がHIVポジティブということも珍しくはない。だから、寝たきりの人たちの多くは、自分がエイズである事を知っている。その先に"死"が待ち受けていることも…。
そしてここでもう一つの問題が浮上する。それは、両親を失くした子供たちが孤児になってしまうことだ。その中には母子感染により生まれた時からAIDSに感染している子供も少なくない。孤児院の数も全く足りていない。子供たちの将来にも暗い影を差しかけている。

現在、私達African JAG Projectでは、無医村地域におけるVCTの実施（HIVの血液検査）、国立病院までのトランスポート・クーポンの配布とプライベート・ホスピタルでの無料診療クーポンの配布、孤児院への食糧支援を行っている。最近のAIDSの薬はとても効力が高く、ステージ3で歩行できないような人でも薬をきちんと飲み、栄養を取れば自足歩行ができるようになり、働くことも可能になる。そうなれば、孤児の数も急激に増えることはない。だから取りあえず病院へ行き、薬を常用するということが大切だと私達は考えている。
アフリカの子供たちの笑顔には特別なものがある。お金も食料も水さえもない中であの子供たちの笑顔だけが唯一の"光"。その"光"を失くさないために一人でも多くの人にこの現実を知って欲しい。そして自分の出来ることから何かを始めて欲しい。同じ地球上にリアルタイムで生きているのだから!!

文：浅野 典子
DJ KRUSHや澤田純（アーティスト）をプロデュースするEs遊Esの代表であり、写真、文筆、映像、音楽、アートの分野でクリエイターとしても活動している。AFRICAN JAG PROJECTでは、アフリカを自らまわり、支援活動を精力的に行っている。1994年以降、アフリカ12ヵ国を通算で約30回訪れ、マラウイへは2006年4月に初めて訪問した後、すでに3度滞在している。

COUNTRY INFORMATION

国名	マラウイ共和国
面積	11.8万km²
人口	1,290万人
首都	リロングウェ
民族	バンツー族（チュワ族、トゥンブーカ族、ンゴニ族、ヤオ族など）
言語	チュワ語、英語（以上公用語）、各部族語
宗教	キリスト教、イスラム教、伝統宗教
独立記念日	1964年7月6日

ラゴスから車で北へ3時間程走ったところに、オショボという町がある。ナイジェリア第3の州都、毎年8月に行われる"オシュン・フェスティバル"はとても有名で、この時期オショボには世界中からアフリカ好きの人々が集まる。王様のパラスから選ばれた処女の娘が頭に生贄を載せて"女神"が祀られているオシュン寺院へと約2kmの道のりを歩く。そのあとをオシュン州のあちこちから集まったドラム・マスターやダンス・マスター、着飾った人々が続く。あちこちでアフリカン・ドラムがリズムを刻み、とてもエキサイティングで感動的なお祭りだ。最終地点、オシュン寺院には祭りのときにしか見ることができない"女神"の他に、数百年前に描かれた壁画や現代作家の自然木を使った立像など様々なアートが存在する。その独特な形はピカソやマティスがアフリカン・アートに大きな影響を受けたということが一瞬で納得出来てしまうほどである。

オショボには数多くのアーティストが存在している。1962年にオーストリア出身のウリ・バウアーがこの地にフリー・スクールのような施設を開設したことにより、黒人の持つ独特の感性が開花し、自由で独自性を持つアートが次々に生み出されていった。そして現在は、オショボ派としてアフリカン・アートの中でも1、2を争う存在になっている。オショボ派のアーティスト達が面白いのは、それぞれがそれぞれの手法を持ち、オリジナリティ溢れる作品を作り出していることだと思う。普通、同じエリアのアーティストの手法は似てきてしまうものだが、ここの人たちは皆それぞれに独自の手法を持ち、全く違った絵を描き出す。バティック、刺し子、ビーズ、藍染め、油絵、版画…等々。ヨーロッパナイズもアメリカナイズもされていない、独特の色彩感覚でアフリカの民話の中に存在していそうな変な生き物を描いているオショボ派のアーティストたちの作品は実に魅力的だ。

ナイジェリアという国は、音楽やアートに関しては本当に面白く、才能が溢れている。何度もナイジェリアを訪れ、その度にエキサイティングなアフリカン・ドラムやダンス、アフリカン・アートに触れてきた。これで、治安が良かったらもっともっと大勢の人が世界中から訪れると思うし、ここに存在する才能も海外に出て行かれるのだと思う。しかし、玄関口であるラゴスの空港職員や警官が賄賂を要求したりするのは日常茶飯事で、強盗も多く、あまりにも危険な要素が多すぎる。以前、唯一安全といわれたシェラトンホテルのレストランでAMEXのゴールド・カードを使った後にいきなりカードを止められたことがあった。問い合わせると私のカードを使ってナイジェリアからアメリカの通信販売会社に大量の注文が入ったのだそうだ。カードを使ったのはこの1回だけ。ともかく"自分の身は自分で守る"が鉄則。隙を見せればそれまで…という感じだ。とはいえ、ナイジェリア人の全てがそういうことでは全くないし、田舎に行けばのどかな時間も流れている。アフリカン・アートやアフリカン・ドラム、アフリカン・ダンスに興味のある人は十分注意して行ってみて欲しい国。でも、私が今までに行ったアフリカ諸国の中で一番危ないと感じたもの事実。ともかくナイジェリアに行く人は決して油断しないで楽しんできて欲しい。

The town called Oshogbo, is a three hour drive north by car from Lagos. This is Nigeria's third provincial capital. At Osun Sacred Grove, a variety of art exists; modern-day artists use natural wood to make statues, but several hundred years ago, artists drew murals. From this unique art form, for a moment one could almost be convinced of the huge influence that Matisse and Picasso received from African art.
There are many artists living in Oshogbo. In 1962, a free-school facility was set up in this area, by an Australian national, Uli Bauer, who brought about the production of a succession of artwork, possessing a free individual uniqueness, and who made Black people's unique sense blossom. Consequently, now Oshogbo style African art is vying for first or second amongst all African art. I think, what is interesting about the Oshogbo artists, is that various artists use a variety of methods, to produce artwork overflowing with originality. Normally, the technique used by artists from the same area is similar, however, here people use a variety of individual methods to create artwork, that is completely different; batik, quilted coats, beads, indigo-dyeing, oil painting, wood block prints, and so on. With a unique sense for colors, without being Europeanized or Americanized, this group of Oshogbo artists, who depict mysterious creatures, which exists in African folktales, are truly charming.

ナイジェリア／オショボ派のアフリカン・アート
AFRICAN ART

COUNTRY INFORMATION

国名	ナイジェリア連邦共和国
面積	92.4万km²
人口	1億4,000万人
首都	アブジャ
民族	ハウサ人、ヨルバ人、イボ人など250民族以上と推定
言語	英語(公用語)、各民族語
宗教	イスラム教、キリスト教、伝統宗教
独立記念日	1960年10月1日

page.117

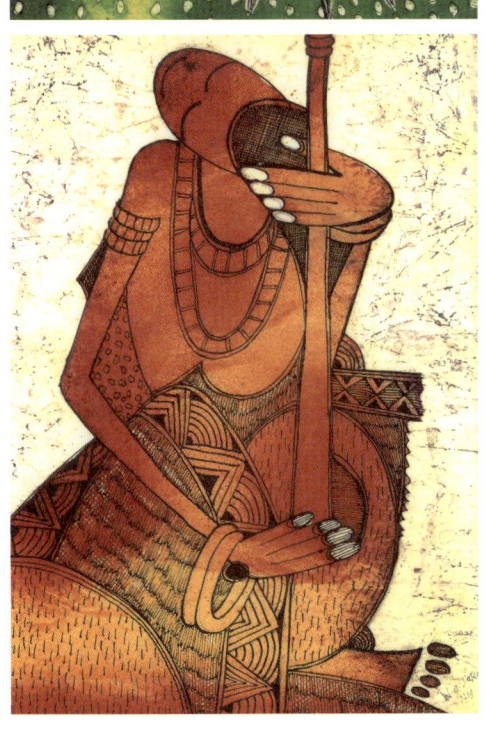

雑誌の定期購読者が増えるごとに、アフリカのケニアに学校舎を寄贈するという企画を実践した『ソトコト』。この斬新な考えはどこから浮かんだのかについて話を聞いた。

+81：この企画の内容と誕生理由を教えてください。
SOTOKOTO（以下S）：月刊ソトコトの定期購読者が2,000人集まるごとに世界の途上国・地域に小学校の校舎がひとつ誕生するという企画を立てました。世界には教育を必要としている子供たちがたくさんいます。ところが、資金不足のために校舎が建てられず、授業が行えなかったり、天候まかせの野外授業のみというところが多いのです。企画の結果、第1回目はケニア・マサイマラ国立保護区に隣接するキリンドーニ村キミンテット小学校に校舎が完成しました。その後、同国立保護区にあるイロクワイア小学校に校舎が完成し、翌年、校舎の隣に雨水を貯めるタンクが完成しました。その他に机の寄贈なども行いました。

+81：なぜケニアで展開しようと考えたのでしょうか？
S：マサイマラ国立保護区にムパタサファリクラブというロッジを経営しており、地域（マサイ）の住民の雇用を行うなど地域と密接に関わっています。その中で、将来のある子供たちに何かサポートできないかと思いついたのが校舎などの建設サポートでした。ただ、建設会社へ依頼するだけでは校舎は出来上がらないため、建設現場をロッジスタッフに立ち合わせ監督もしました。
また、毎年ケニアで野生教室を行っている桐蔭学園の高校生とマサイの小学校生徒との交流にも協力しています。

※尚、現在はCO2排出権付き「ソトコト」定期購読プログラムがスタートしたため、この企画は停止しています。

Profile：ソトコト
小黒一三氏が1999年、環境ライフスタイル雑誌「ソトコト」を創刊。スローライフ、スローフード、ロハスなどをいち早く日本に紹介して、新しい価値観を提案している。

COUNTRY INFORMATION

国名	ケニア共和国
面積	58.3万km²
人口	3,430万人
首都	ナイロビ
民族	キクユ人、ルヒヤ人、カレンジン人、ルオ人など
言語	スワヒリ語、英語
宗教	伝統宗教、キリスト教、イスラム教
独立記念日	1963年12月12日

SOTOKOTO
ソトコト

Editor's Note
旅行後記

今回は、アフリカ最南端都市ケープタウンから、最も危険な都市ヨハネスブルグ、そして動物の宝庫クルーガー国立公園まで、南アフリカ共和国を横断する旅であった。

ケープタウンの印象は、世界でも稀に見る美しい景観を持つ地域であり、ここがアフリカということを忘れてしまうほど優雅なライフスタイルを楽しめるリゾート都市であった。ここでは、他の都市では経験できないコロニアル風の生活様式を味わうことができる。

ヨハネスブルグは、いままで訪れた都市の中で最も危険を感じた街であり、最もエネルギッシュで魅力的に感じた街でもある。わずか2km四方の狭いダウンタウン地域に危険と魅力を兼ね合わせた不思議な都市である。ケープタウンとの違いは、アーティストの作品を比べてみても明らかだ。洗練されたケープタウン在住のアーティスト作品と、エネルギー溢れるヨハネスブルグ在住のアーティスト作品とは全く対照的である。ヨハネスブルグは、強烈なインパクトを与えるエネルギッシュなアフリカらしい都市と言えるだろう。

クルーガー国立公園は、悠久の自然と動物の生態を肌に感じ、胸をワクワクさせながら時を過ごせる。夜明け前に起き、サバンナに出て、陽が沈むとともに帰る。太陽を中心にまわる生活の心地よさを改めて感じる。人間も自然に少しずつ同化していくことを実感する素晴らしい体験ができる。

アフリカは、一度訪れたら何度も訪れたくなる魅力の大地と言われている。北アフリカのモロッコからサハラ砂漠への旅、そして今回の南アフリカ横断の旅は、気候も地形も全く異なる地域でありながら、共通するものがある。それは、壮大な地球の地形と生存するための苛酷な環境が、人間に生きていることを実感させるからである。人間の生存本能をフルに引き出させてくれる場所と言える。

具体的な例を挙げると「生きるための距離間」である。写真でも紹介しているインパラを襲うライオンだが、インパラはライオンの存在を知りつつ、注視しながら草を食べている。ライオンとの距離は、いつ襲われても安全圏と判断しているのだ。結果、飢えたライオンはインパラを捕らえることができなかった。インパラは生きるための距離間を正確に把握しているのである。同じことが危険な都市といわれるヨハネスブルグでもあった。ガイドは、必ず私たちの傍にはおらず10メートルほど離れた場所にいる。最初は気がつかなかったのだが、私たちの周囲全体の様子を見るためであった。危害を加えそうな人の存在を探し、その危険人物と私たちの距離を目測しているのだ。危険を予見し、阻止するために必要な距離間を保っていたのだ。

全てが非日常生活であり、出会うもの全てに胸を躍らせ、神経を鋭敏にさせる。この緊張感こそが、アフリカの旅を楽しませてくれるのだろう。平穏な日常生活に慣れた私たちに心地よい刺激を与えてくれる。子供のとき夢見たジャングルで動物に出会う旅は、想像するより安易であった。ほんの少しの勇気と冒険心を持てば、動物達との出会いがそこに待っている。

Voyageのテーマは、「1週間、机の上で苦悩するならば、旅に出よう。たった1週間の旅の刺激が創造するものを変えてしまう」である。ひとりの人間が頭の中で考えることなど、たかが知れている。旅に出ることにより、多くの刺激と経験を体得できる。キャッチボールでボールを捕らえたグラブの感触や自転車のペダルを踏む感触など、一度体得すると一生忘れることがないのと同じである。私自身も初めて海外に旅して踏みしめたアテネの土の感触を忘れることはない。生きていることを実感し、世の中を別の角度から見ることにより視野も広がる。机の上では、解決しないことや知り得なかったことが分かる。旅は人生を大きく変える道標である。さあ、いますぐ旅の計画をはじめよう。

Editor in Chief / Creative Director　山下 悟

+81 Voyage Edition

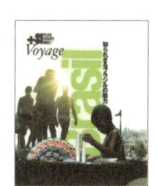

+81 Voyage
Brazil issue
¥1,200 (税抜)

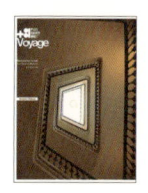

+81 Voyage
Barcelona issue
from Spain to Morocco
¥1,500 (税抜)

+81 Voyage
Scandinavia issue
A journey in design
¥1,500 (税抜)

Credit

Editor in Chief
Satoru Yamashita
satoru@dd-wave.co.jp

Editors
Kyoko Ishima
Masayo Fukaya
Kazuhiro Hasegawa
Hazuki Itoya
Natsumi Suzuki
Miwa Tanaka

Photographer
Kazuyo Kawatoko

Translators
R.I.C. Publications
Luke Baker

Proofreaders
Jez Smadja
Luke Baker

Creative & Art Director
Satoru Yamashita

Designers
Kiichiro Yamasaki (p6-13)
Kouichi Ishikawa (p16-47, p84-87)
Noriyuki Ueda (p48-83, p105-109)
Yukiko Takashima (p88-104)
Yoshinori Hozumi (p110-120)

SPECIAL THANKS

Cape Town
Deborah Weber
Nicole Moody
Karen Richards
Udo Bartsch

Johannesburg
Marcus Neustetter
Leigh-Anne Niehaus

Tokyo
Akiko Nishimura
Ayako Uragami
Tomomi Goto
Kristen Heyburgh
Ryuta Kudo
Seiji Yabushita
Takashi Kimura

Embassy of Sweden
(Joachim Bergström)
British Council
(Chika Sudo)
Switzerland Tourism
(Masayo Oshio)
MEK/Finnish Tourist Board
(Shigeyoshi Noto)
Netherlands Board of Tourism & Convention
(Tomomi Tsukakoshi, Harue Nakagawa)
National Tourist Office of Spain (Tae Mito)
Goethe-Institut Japan Doitsu Bunka Kaikan
(Noriko Horiguchi)

Printing Director
Katsuyuki Watanabe
(Prise Communication)

Printing Manager
Shigeru Sato
(Prise Communication)

Publisher
Satoru Yamashita

+81 Voyage South Africa issue
発行日 2007年10月30日
発行人 山下 悟
発行所／編集 ディー・ディー・ウェーブ株式会社
107-0062 東京都港区南青山2-22-2 クインビル6F
TEL 03 5411 5725　FAX 03 5414 5326

PUBLISHER : SATORU YAMASHITA
PUBLISHED and EDITED By D.D.WAVE CO.,LTD
2-22-2 MINAMI AOYAMA, MINATO-KU, TOKYO JAPAN
TEL +81 3 5411 5725　FAX +81 3 5414 5236

+81 infomation
E-MAIL plus81@dd-wave.co.jp
WEB http://www.plus81.com　http://www.plus81.com/voyage

発売元 株式会社河出書房新社
151-0051 東京都渋谷区千駄ヶ谷2-32-2　TEL 03 3404 1201

印刷所 株式会社プライズコミュニケーション

OVERSEAS DISTRIBUTER
NIPPAN IPS CO., LTD
113-0034
1-3-4 YUSHIMA, BUNKYO-KU, TOKYO JAPAN
TEL +81 3 5802 1852　FAX +81 3 5802 1891
E-MAIL magazine@clubjapan.jp

Printed in Japan

©2007 D.D.WAVE CO.,LTD. All rights reserved.
Reproduction in whole or in part without permission is prohibited.
本書の収録内容の無断転載、複写、引用等を禁じます。

ISBN 978-4-309-90744-4

協力

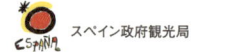